HEADSTART

TEACHER'S BOOK   **BEGINNER**

Tim Falla

OXFORD UNIVERSITY PRESS

CONTENTS

INTRODUCTION

Headstart is a short foundation course for adult and young adult absolute beginners. It introduces, gradually and methodically, basic grammar and vocabulary to prepare students for *Headway Elementary* and other elementary courses.

Headstart covers language points from the first five units of *Headway Elementary*, and areas of vocabulary from the first nine units. If your beginners have progressed easily through the material in *Headstart*, then, if they move on to *Headway Elementary*, they could probably begin at Unit 3. Or you may like to begin *Headway Elementary* at Unit 1 but concentrate on the functional language and skills work, which will be new to them. However, if the students need further consolidation of the basic language points covered in *Headstart*, then they can start *Headway Elementary* at Unit 1.

How to use the course

The organization of *Headstart* is similar to that of *Headway Elementary* and *Pre-intermediate*. Each unit starts with a Presentation of new language followed by a Practice section. Skills work follows, with regular Reading and/or Listening sections, and then a Vocabulary and/or Pronunciation section. Next, there is an Everyday English section and finally a Grammar Summary.

PRESENTATION

New language points and vocabulary are presented in context through texts which students can read and hear at the same time. This enables students to relate the spelling to the sounds of English, and helps with pronunciation, as well as form and use.

You can vary the presentations if you like. Sometimes it is useful to play the cassette first while the students look at the picture with the text covered. Then, after that, they can read and listen. This method may be useful for some non-European students who are not very familiar with Roman script.

When introducing a new item of language, stop and practise pronunciation when students have grasped the meaning. A lot of the presentation material is recorded to allow pronunciation practice. With single words or short phrases, there is a long enough pause in the recording for students to listen and repeat before the next item. For longer phrases and sentences, there is a long enough pause in the recording to allow you to pause the tape manually and ask students to repeat.

Do not stint on practice and revision. Although 'Listen and repeat' may not seem the most exciting of exercises to the teacher, it is important to give the students ample opportunity to get their mouths round new vocabulary and unfamiliar language. It also helps students to internalize it and recall it later, as well as building their confidence. (See next section, 'Teaching beginners – tips and techniques', for more details on listening and repeating.)

> ⚠️ The caution box is used to highlight areas of potential confusion. Stop and go over the information with the students.

PRACTICE

This section contains a variety of controlled and freer practice exercises, often involving all four skills. Wherever possible, the opportunity for pairwork and personalization is provided. The Workbook contains further practice exercises, including more emphasis on personalized writing activities.

Pairwork, and sometimes groupwork, is an important feature of the course. Working with their peers gives students extra help and support, and increases student talking time. Even if students are doing a writing exercise, they can work together to complete it, or at least compare their answers before you check answers with the whole class.

SKILLS WORK

A feature of *Headstart* is the introduction of simple skills work from the beginning.

Listening There are regular unseen listening sections, in dialogue or monologue form. These provide further practice of the language of the unit and, later in the course, help to develop students' ability to understand the main message of a listening text.

Reading Regular graded reading passages also provide further practice in the target language of the units in a wider context, as well as developing students' reading comprehension abilities. At the beginning of the course, the language in the readings is tightly controlled and graded, and only one or two words will be unknown to the students. As the course progresses, the readings become longer, with slightly more unfamiliar vocabulary in the texts. This gives students practice in dealing with new words and prepares them for the longer reading texts in *Headway Elementary*.

Speaking and Pronunciation There are a variety of speaking activities. In the Presentation sections, students have the opportunity to practise the pronunciation and intonation of new language. In the Practice sections, more controlled speaking tasks lead to freer speaking activities, e.g. information gaps and questionnaires.

Speech bubbles give the students examples of the language needed to complete a task and are there to help you set up the activity.

There are also simple Pronunciation sections throughout the book that highlight word-stress patterns.

VOCABULARY

There is a strong lexical syllabus in *Headstart*, and the vocabulary is carefully graded and recycled throughout so that the students don't suffer from overloading. A lexical set is introduced and practised alongside the main grammar point in the Presentation sections. Vocabulary exercises are also a regular feature of the Practice sections, where the emphasis is on revision of vocabulary learnt up to that point. Here, students are asked to sort, categorize, and match vocabulary items. Similar exercises are to be found in the Workbook.

There is a Word List for each unit at the back of the Student's Book and students are encouraged to translate and learn the vocabulary.

EVERYDAY ENGLISH

As well as a grammar and lexical syllabus, *Headstart* has a simple functional syllabus. This section introduces functional language in useful situations for the students to listen to and practise, and survival English such as spelling, numbers, telling the time, and days.

GRAMMAR SUMMARY

The grammar is presented in tabular form at the end of each unit, along with an exercise for students to check their understanding. Prepositions and functional phrases are also listed.

REVISION

There are two Stop and Check revision sections (after Units 6 and 12), which allow students to check their progress in grammar, vocabulary, reading, listening, speaking, and writing.

WORKBOOK

This provides a variety of practice exercises to consolidate and extend the language and vocabulary presented in class, including simple free writing exercises. It also offers two further Stop and Check revision sections, after Units 6 and 12, for students to check their progress.

STUDENT'S CASSETTE

This is an optional accompaniment to the Workbook. The exercises in the Workbook marked with a tapescript number (e.g. **T5**) are recorded on cassette for the students to listen, check, and repeat. The student's cassette is ideal for any student wanting to hear English outside the classroom, and particularly beneficial to students who lack confidence in speaking and who have listening and/or pronunciation problems. The cassette is optional and all the exercises in the Workbook can be completed without it.

TEACHING BEGINNERS — TIPS AND TECHNIQUES

1 A STEP-BY-STEP APPROACH

Beginners require a very careful, staged approach with plenty of repetition, practice, and revision to help them internalize new language and to give them confidence. Suggested stages are as follows:

• Presentation of language point

See the previous section, 'How to use the course'.

• Listening and repeating (drilling)

You can use the cassette as a model, or provide the model yourself for this activity. Allow the students to listen to the word, phrase, or sentence two or three times before you ask them to repeat it. For example, to drill the sentence *How are you?* play the cassette and/or model the sentence yourself two or three times using the same pronunciation and intonation, then ask the students as a class to repeat the phrase (i.e. choral drilling). Don't say it with them, but instead listen to what they are saying. Say *Again* for them to repeat a second time. If it sounds as if they have got it right, ask one or two students individually to say it again for you to check (i.e. individual drilling). If the choral repetition *doesn't* sound right, remodel the phrase for students to listen to again, then have them repeat chorally again, before moving on to individual drilling.

• Practice

Move carefully from controlled to freer practice. Beginners require plenty of practice in order (1) to get their mouths round new language and vocabulary, and (2) to internalize it and remember it. Don't stint on practice or revision, but equally do not spend too long on any one thing, or the students may get bored and switch off. You can always come back later and do more work on it.

The following techniques ensure enough practice as well as variety.

Pairwork

A lot of work can be done in pairs. Open and closed pairwork are often referred to in the teaching notes.

Open pairwork

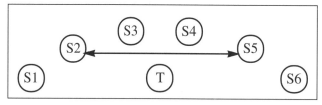

As a stage after drilling and before closed pairwork, you can call on two students at a time to practise the lines of a dialogue, ask and answer a question, etc. across the room, with the rest of the class listening.

Do open pairwork:

- to set up and demonstrate a closed pairwork activity
- to check understanding of a task
- to check students' grammar, pronunciation, and intonation before they go on to closed pairwork
- after a closed pairwork activity or a written exercise to check performance of the task.

Don't call on the whole class to perform open pairwork. Two or three pairs of students, each performing one or two exchanges, should be sufficient to check language. More than this may make the activity drag and become boring.

Closed pairwork

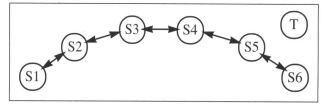

With closed pairwork, students talk and listen only to each other. This gives them more speaking time and a chance to practise with a peer without having to 'perform' in front of you and the class. It is important, though, for you to go round and listen to and monitor students' performances unobtrusively. This will help you to identify persistent errors and misunderstandings. Do not interrupt and correct students while you are going round unless absolutely necessary, as this inhibits fluency. Instead, make a note of persistent errors as you monitor. Then, afterwards, you can put some of the errors on the board for the students to correct. (It is probably not necessary to identify the culprits!)

Chain practice

This is a good way of using flashcards in a practice speaking activity. It offers variety, a change of pace, and a lot of practice of the language point without becoming boring. The following example describes a way of using flashcards of famous people.

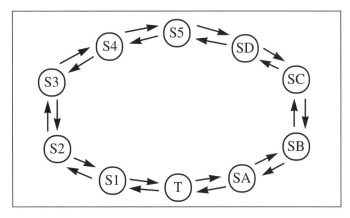

1 Stand in a circle with the students, with the flashcards in your hand.
2 Turn to S1 on your left, show the first card and ask a question, e.g. *What's his/her name?* S1 answers, and receives the flashcard from you.
3 S1 then turns to S2 and asks the same question. S2 answers, and receives card.
4 While S1 is asking S2, turn to SA on your right, show the second card, and ask the question *What's his/her name?* SA answers, receives the card, and turns and asks SB.
5 While SA is asking SB, turn back to S1 again with the third flashcard, and ask the same question.
6 Continue the process until all the flashcards are in circulation and the students are asking and answering. There will probably be a bottleneck when the student opposite you starts getting questions from both sides at once, but it's part of the fun. Eventually the flashcards should all come back to you. This practice game can get fast and furious!

2 CLASSROOM PRACTICES

Whether you have a monolingual or a multilingual class, it will save a great deal of time and effort if, at the beginning, you set up clear classroom practices and establish familiar routines. This will quickly provide comfort and reassurance for beginners who can find it nerve-racking to deal with a new and alien language. Also, many complete beginners are adults who haven't been in the classroom for a long time, and whose previous experience of learning a language was probably very different.

Classroom language
You could spend a little time at the beginning pre-teaching some useful classroom language (e.g. *Sorry, I don't understand.*, *Can you spell it, please?*) and instructions (e.g. *Work in pairs*, *Read*, *Listen*, *Repeat*, *All together*, *Again*, *Homework*, etc). Some basic classroom language for students is introduced in Unit 4, but you might want to teach it earlier.

Numbers and the alphabet are introduced very early so that you can refer students to page and exercise numbers in English, and spell words for them. All of this will enable you to keep an 'English' atmosphere.

When having to give instructions for an activity, rehearse them beforehand so that they are simple, clear and concise, and *demonstrate*, rather than explain wherever possible. Avoid repeating yourself or overexplaining, as it tends only to create further confusion.

Explaining new vocabulary
Explanation of new vocabulary to beginners can be problematic, particularly in multilingual classes, and/or where you have no knowledge of the students' mother tongue.

Make sure the students have a simple bilingual dictionary. Use pictures and/or draw on the board whenever possible. Do not worry if you are not a brilliant artist. Simple line drawings are very quick and effective. Start collecting flashcards, posters, photos, etc. to help you.

Example sentences with the new word in context are often better than explanations (unless the explanations are very simple). Giving a similar word or the opposite can also be useful, e.g. *finish = stop*, *get up ≠ go to bed*.

Pronunciation of new vocabulary
When you introduce new vocabulary, make sure you drill the pronunciation of the words as well. This should be done after the meaning has been established so that students are not mouthing words that they do not understand. It is also a good idea to get yourself into the habit of highlighting and marking up on the board the main stress of new words, and having students copy this down, e.g. téacher or <u>tea</u>cher

Use of mother tongue
There can be no doubt that it is useful to *know* the students' own language (L1), especially if you have a monolingual class. Whether or not or how much you *use* it is another matter. It is probably best to use it sparingly:

● Perhaps in the first lesson talk to students in L1 about the course, how they will work, etc. and explain that you will be using English with them.
● Perhaps use L1 to check instructions for a new and unfamiliar activity, or to check understanding of a new language point, but only after using English.
● You can use L1 for translation of new vocabulary (where there is a one-to-one, direct translation) and to deal with students' queries, particularly when it would waste a lot of time trying to explain in English.

Otherwise, you may find that if beginners feel it is acceptable to use their own language freely in the classroom, they are inhibited from taking the plunge and speaking English to you and to each other, and it becomes more difficult for them to make that important leap.

UNIT 1

you – my/your – This is ... – is/are – What? – Numbers 1–20

Introduction to the Unit

This unit presents basic greetings in a formal and informal setting, some fairly international words, and a first introduction to numbers.

Notes on the Unit

PRESENTATION

1 This presentation introduces the language of basic greetings. It also provides a way for you and the students to learn each other's names.

a **T1** Point to the first picture in the Student's Book. You could point to the two characters in turn and say *This is Ann. This is Luc.* Play the first exchange and tell the students to follow in their books.

If the students are non-European and/or have script difficulties, you could have them listen to the cassette once or twice without reading, and then have them listen and read the text at the same time.

Introduce the second picture and dialogue in the same way, and then play the dialogue.

b **T1** Use the 'Listen and repeat' sections to focus on pronunciation and intonation.

Play the first line *Hello. My name's Ann.* Pause the cassette and ask students to repeat. You may like to model the sentence again yourself before or after they repeat. Encourage an accurate voice range. (Many languages do not use such a wide voice range as English so this needs to be actively encouraged.) Have the students repeat each line twice chorally, and then ask students to repeat lines individually. Follow the same procedure with the rest of the dialogue.

The second dialogue is slightly different. It is more formal, giving surnames as well as first names, and the reply is *My name's ...* Play each line and have the students repeat chorally and individually.

c Ask students around the class *What's your name?* and have them answer *My name's ...*

d Start off the mingling exercise yourself by going up to a student, introducing yourself and asking their name. Have the students follow suit. You may like to encourage them to shake hands as they introduce themselves, particularly if they don't know one another.

After the students have completed the activity and sat down, ask one student to go round the class saying everyone's name while the other students help if need be, to test their memories. (You might want to do this yourself, too, to make sure you have remembered all the students' names!)

2a **T2** Students look at the photograph and then read and listen to the text.

b **T2** Students repeat line by line, chorally and individually. Pay attention to pronunciation and intonation.

c/d **T3** Students follow the same procedure as in **a** and **b** above with the second dialogue.

e Have two students come up and join you at the front of the class to demonstrate this exchange first. Introduce the students to each other. Have them shake hands while saying *Hello.*

Put the students into groups of three. Have each student take it in turn to introduce the other two. Go round the class to monitor while they are doing this. Depending on the class, when the activity is over, you may like to ask one or two groups to go through the dialogue again while the whole class listens.

3a **T4** Students look at the photograph and then read and listen to the dialogue.

b **T4** Students repeat after the cassette or after you, concentrating on pronunciation and intonation.

c/d **T5** Repeat the procedure in **a** and **b** above with the second dialogue.

e Ask individual students *How are you?* to elicit the answer *Fine/Very well, thanks. And you?* Reply yourself in turn. Make sure students realize that *And you?* requires an answer *Fine/Very well, thanks.*

Then get students to ask and answer you and each other in open pairs across the class. It may be helpful to gesture to your partner when you say *And you?* to aid comprehension.

f This is another class mingling activity. (You may like to develop a gesture which means 'mingle'.) Stand up with the students and demonstrate with one or two before telling the students to circulate. The activity gives students another chance to use and practise one another's names as well.

PRACTICE

1a You may like to write the first dialogue gap-fill on the board and do it with the whole class, as they may not be accustomed to this kind of exercise. Encourage them not to refer back to the complete dialogues on the previous pages.

Write students' suggestions (right or wrong) in the gaps.

b **T1** Play the dialogue for them to listen and check. See if they can hear and correct any mistakes themselves before you offer correction.

Answers	
Ann	Hello. My *name's* Ann. What's *your* name?
Luc	Luc.
David	*Hello.* My name's David Wilson. *What's* your *name*?
María	*My* name's María Oliván.

c/d **T4** and **T5** If the first dialogue was completed satisfactorily, you could put students in pairs to try and complete the second and third dialogues together. Go round and monitor, but don't correct any mistakes yet.

Have students listen and check before you correct mistakes with the class.

Answers	
Luc	*Hi,* Ann. *How* are you?
Ann	Fine, thanks, Luc. *And you?*
Luc	Fine, *thanks.*

David	*How are* you, María ?
María	*Fine*, thanks. *And you?*
David	*Very well*, thanks.

2a/b **T6** It is probably best to play the dialogue twice before students try and order it. Let them check their ideas with each other, then write their version(s) on the board and have them listen again and check.

Answers
Correct order: 3, 6, 4, 1, 5, 2.

3 In pairs, students write out the sentences with the words in the correct order. Check their answers.

Answers
1   What's your name?
2   This is Ann.
3   How are you?
4   My name's Sylvia.

Additional material

Workbook Unit 1
Exercises 1, 2, 4, and 5 These provide further greetings and introductions practice.

VOCABULARY

English words

1a Many of these words may be known to the students as they are fairly international. Have students work in pairs or groups of three to match them to the pictures. Check their answers and elicit/model and practise the pronunciation of the words before moving on to **1b**.

You might like to start straight away marking the stress on new words on the board to show that English is stress-timed (e.g. hospital). If you prefer to leave this for the time being, it is done from Unit 3 onwards.

Answers	
a supermarket	a video
a hospital	football
a photograph	a radio
a telephone	a cinema
tennis	a television
a cassette	a hamburger

b Demonstrate the activity with a good student. In pairs, students take it in turns to point to a picture and have their partner give them the word.

> **Additional idea**
>
> You may like to teach students the phrases *What's this? It's a …*, or simply *This is (a) …* if you think they will be able to manage them. (They have already used the phrase *This is …* to introduce people.) Say *What's this?* and point to a picture. Students can either just say what it is, *a radio, tennis*, etc., or reply with *It's (a) …*

Students then take it in turns to point at the pictures and elicit answers in pairs as further practice.

c Students may come up with their own 'international' words or cognates with their own language. Put them on the board and practise the pronunciation. Unless you know the students' native language, explaining such vocabulary can be tricky, and you may be reduced to drawing or miming.

> **Additional material**
> **Workbook Unit 1**
> **Exercise 3** This provides further vocabulary practice.

EVERYDAY ENGLISH
Numbers 1–20

Numbers 1–10 are introduced in **Exercise 1**, and 11–20 in **Exercise 2**.

Often students are already quite familiar with 1–10 and you can go straight on to introduce 11–20. If this is the case, you could skip the number dictation in **1d** and include numbers 1–10 in the dictation in **2d**.

If students have difficulty with 1–10, then you may like to leave 11–20 for the next lesson, and revise 1–10 at that point as well.

> **Suggestion**
>
> From now on, use numbers as much as possible when referring to exercise and page numbers for extra practice. Continue to do quick number revisions in future lessons.

1a **T7** Students read and listen to the numbers.

b **T7** Students listen and repeat each number after the cassette or after you. Write *eight* on the board and put

a stroke through the *g* to show that it is silent. Count round the class, with each student saying their number a couple of times to check pronunciation and to aid memory.

If students are really unfamiliar with the words, you may like to let them practise counting by themselves for a while, before you move on.

c Write figures at random on the board. Students say the numbers as you write.

d Give students a number dictation. Say numbers at random, writing them down yourself so that you have a means of checking. Students write the figures, not the words, as you say them. Have one student read their list of numbers out to correct.

2a **T8** Students read and listen to the numbers.

b **T8** Students repeat each number after the cassette or after you. As in **1b** above, count round the class from 11.

c Write numbers at random on the board for students to say.

d Give students a number dictation, as described in **1d** above.

e **T9** Students listen to the numbers on the cassette and tick the one they hear in each row. You can demonstrate by writing the first row on the board, playing the cassette and ticking 12.

Play the cassette through, twice if necessary, then check students' answers.

> **Answers**
> 12, 15, 18, 7, 13

f Students prepare a list of random figures (between 1 and 20) to dictate to their partner. They take it in turns to dictate their list. The student who is taking down the dictated numbers writes the figures, not the words, and then reads the list back to their partner to check the answers. You may need to demonstrate this using the board and a student partner, unless you can explain in the students' native language.

> **Additional material**
> **Workbook Unit 1**
> **Exercises 6, 7, and 8** These provide further practice of numbers.

GRAMMAR SUMMARY

This is a whole-class activity. Read through the substitution tables with the students. Indicate *my* and *your* with appropriate gestures. You may like to have students close their books, and you write the tables on the board. You could leave gaps and elicit the answers for some of the substitution items, e.g. for 1 or 2 you could write up *my* but elicit *your*.

Then either do the **Exercise** as a class, with students joining in to suggest answers for the gaps, or have students work in pairs and then check the answers with the whole class.

> **Answers**
> 1 My name *is* Linda.
> 2 How *are* you?
> 3 This *is* a video.
> 4 What *is* your name?

Word List

Ask the students to turn to page 75 and go through the words with them. Ask them to learn the words for homework, and test them on a few in the following lesson.

> **Additional material**
> **Workbook Unit 1**
> **Exercise 9** This is a word search of vocabulary and grammar words introduced in the unit.
> **Exercise 10** In this exercise students translate sentences containing the main grammar points presented in the unit.

UNIT 1 TAPESCRIPTS

Tapescript 1

Ann	Hello. My name's Ann. What's your name?
Luc	Luc.
David	Hello. My name's David Wilson. What's your name?
María	My name's María Oliván.

Tapescript 2

David	John, this is María Oliván. María, this is John Black.
John	Hello, María.
María	Hello, John.

Tapescript 3

Ann	Luc, this is Jane. Jane, this is Luc.
Luc	Hello, Jane.
Jane	Hello, Luc.

Tapescript 4

Luc	Hi, Ann. How are you?
Ann	Fine, thanks, Luc. And you?
Luc	Fine, thanks.

Tapescript 5

David	How are you, María?
María	Fine, thanks. And you?
David	Very well, thanks.

Tapescript 6

Julie	Hello. My name's Julie. What's your name?
María	My name's María.
Sandra	Hello, Julie. How are you?
Julie	Fine, thanks. Sandra, this is María.
Sandra	Hello, María.
María	Hello, Sandra.

Tapescript 7

one	three	five	seven	nine
two	four	six	eight	ten

Tapescript 8

eleven	thirteen	fifteen	seventeen	nineteen
twelve	fourteen	sixteen	eighteen	twenty

Tapescript 9

twelve	fifteen	eighteen	seven	thirteen

UNIT 2

Countries – *his/her* – *I/you/he/she* – *am* – *Where?* – Alphabet

Introduction to the Unit

This unit introduces some countries, along with the third person for names, and *Where are you/is s/he from?* The alphabet is introduced and a there is a short reading comprehension.

Notes on the Unit

PRESENTATION

1a Draw students' attention to the photos of Luc and Ann who appeared in Unit 1. Read the sentences *His name's Luc. Her name's Ann.* aloud to the students. You might like to write them on the board as well, circling *his* and *her* and indicating male and female, before having students go on to gap-fill the other four sentences. Students can do this alone and check their answers in pairs, or work in pairs before you go over the answers with the class.

Answers
1 *Her* name's María.   2 *Her* name's Yoko.
3 *His* name's Carlo.   4 *His name's* Jim.

b **T 10** This introduces the question form. Students read and listen to the cassette.

c **T 10** Students repeat each line after the cassette or after you.

d Go through the photographs yourself first asking *What's his/her name?* and eliciting the answers, before getting students to do the same in pairs.

e Point to a few students and ask the class *What's his/her name?* Then have students practise the questions and answers in open pairs across the class before they ask and answer each other in closed pairs.

Additional idea

You could bring in pictures of famous people for further practice. This would be particularly useful if the concept of *his* and *her* differs in the students' own language. You could use them for open pairwork, or you could try a question and answer chain as follows:

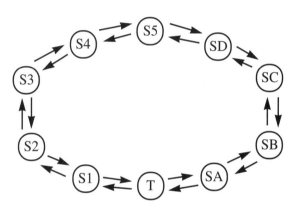

1 Stand in a circle with the students, with the pictures in your hand.
2 Turn to S1 on your left, show the first card and ask *What's his/her name?* S1 answers, and receives the picture from you.
3 S1 then turns to S2 and asks the same question. S2 answers, and receives picture.
4 While S1 is asking S2, turn to SA on your right, show the second picture, and ask the question *What's his/her name?* SA answers, receives the picture, and turns and asks SB.
5 While SA is asking SB, turn back to S1 again with the third picture, and ask the question.
6 Continue the process until all the pictures are in circulation and the students are asking and answering. There will probably be a bottleneck when the student opposite you starts getting questions from both sides at once, but that's part of the fun. Eventually the pictures should all come back to you.

2a In pairs, students try to match the countries with the maps. Go over the answers with them.

Answers	
Japan	France
Italy	Spain
the United States	England

b `T11` Students practise the names of the countries, repeating after you or the cassette. Pay particular attention to stress.

c Students can further practise pronunciation in pairs, pointing to the maps and saying the names of the countries.

3a `T12` This dialogue introduces the second person question form. Students read and listen to the dialogue.

b `T12` Students repeat each line after the cassette. Pay particular attention to intonation, and to the contrastive stress in the second question *Where are you from?* Have students practise the dialogue in open and closed pairs.

c If you have a multilingual class, make sure that all the students' countries are written on the board and practised beforehand. If you have a monolingual class, you might like to teach them *I'm from* (town) *in* (country) to vary the answers.

Students stand up and go round the class, asking and answering each other.

4a This exercise presents the same *I'm from …* statement in the third person and draws attention to the contrast between *His name's …* and *He's from …* You can read the first two sentences aloud with the students before they write the exercise. Alternatively, you can do the whole exercise orally first, focusing students' attention on the photos and maps and asking the questions *What's his/her name?* and *Where's he/she from?* for each person. Then students can go back and write the answers.

Answers
3 Her name's María. She's *from Spain.*
4 His name's Carlo. He's *from Italy.*
5 *Her* name's Yoko. *She's from Japan.*
6 *His* name's Jim. *He's from the United States.*

b/c `T13` Students are now asked to focus on the third person question form. Let them listen to the cassette once or twice before repeating. Pay attention to pronunciation and intonation. Have students practise in open and closed pairs.

PRACTICE

1 Students go back to **Exercise 4a** and ask and answer in pairs about the six people.

> **Additional idea**
>
> If you have pictures of famous people of different nationalities, you can use these for further practice. If not, you can write on the board the names of some famous people whose nationalities students will know, for further question and answer practice.

2a `T14` This is a short dialogue and the students' first short unseen listening. Students should be well prepared for the language it contains by now. Play the cassette as many times as is necessary. The cassette introduces a common European name, Lídia, but non-Europeans may have difficulty with it. If your students fall into this category, just check that they have picked up the sounds correctly and write it on the board for them.

Answers
Name *Lídia*
Country *Spain*

b This exercise provides further practice by giving students a new name and nationality. Make a photocopy of page 64 of the Teacher's Book. The cards provide a male and a female name from each of the countries in the Student's Book and also from the six countries introduced in Exercises 2 and 3 in Unit 2 of the Workbook (Hungary, Turkey, Brazil, Wales, Scotland, Ireland, and England.) You can either just use the cards with the countries introduced in the Student's Book, or pre-teach the other countries using the Workbook.

Cut out the role cards and give them out to the students, telling them this is their new name and country.

c Ask students to stand up and go round the class asking and answering the questions in the speech bubbles. Tell them they must try to remember everyone's new name and country.

d When students have finished and sat down again, indicate one or two students and ask the class *What's his/her name?* and *Where's he/she from?* If the class is good, you can also check with the student in question whether the class has remembered correctly, asking *Is that right?*, and having them answer *Yes* or *No*.

Students continue asking and answering about each other.

3 This is the first information gap exercise that students have encountered in the book, and it therefore needs careful setting up. If possible, explain using the students' own language or demonstrate with a good student yourself first.

Students work in pairs. Each student has the name and nationality of four of the eight people in the photos. The aim is for each student to find out about the other four by asking their partner. Students can refer to each photo by pointing or by saying the number.

While the students are asking and answering about the people in the photos, go round monitoring and helping out. Don't worry if the students show each other their books to spell the names, as the names may cause problems for some nationalities. When they have finished, you can check by asking individual students to tell you about one of the people in the photos. Say *Tell me about number one.*, etc.

Answers
Tell students to look at each other's pages.

Additional material
Workbook Unit 2
Exercise 1 This provides further practice of the countries introduced in the Student's Book.
Exercises 2 and 3 These introduce more countries.
Exercise 4 This provides further practice of all the countries.
Exercise 5 This practises questions and answers in the third person.

READING

This is the first reading text that the students have encountered in the book.

a First ask students to read through the text on their own. Then you can read it with them, explaining any new words. Words and phrases not previously introduced are *doctor*, *teacher*, *school*, *in the centre of*, and *too*. These may prove more difficult for non-European students. *Hospital* appeared in Unit 1. *Teacher*, *school*, and *student* should be easy to explain in the context of the classroom. To explain *doctor*, you can turn to page 14 of the Student's Book (the start of Unit 3), where there is a picture of a doctor. *In the centre of* can be illustrated on the board, and *too* can

be explained by pointing to two students and saying, e.g. *Luc is from France. Pierre is from France, too.*

If you speak the students' L1, you can ask them what the word is in their language to check comprehension.

b In pairs, students complete the sentences from the text. Go over the answers by asking individual students to read out their completed sentences.

Answers
1 Gianni is from *Italy*.
2 He is a *teacher*.
3 His school is in *the centre of Milan*.
4 Heike is from *Germany*.
5 She is a *doctor*.
6 Her hospital is in *the centre of Milan*.

Additional material
Workbook Unit 2
Exercise 8 This provides further reading practice.

EVERYDAY ENGLISH

This offers a short introduction to the alphabet and spelling. Once students have learnt the alphabet, opportunities should be taken to spell new words to the students and to have students spell words in class. In the Everyday English section of Unit 4, students are taught, *Can you spell it, please?* You may like to teach this phrase earlier.

1a **T 15** The letters of the alphabet are arranged according to sound. Draw students' attention to this. Play the cassette while the students follow in their books.

b **T 15** Play the cassette again, stopping at the end of each line for the students to repeat. Then let them practise on their own and in pairs for a while.

c Write the alphabet on the board. Point to each letter in order, and ask students to say it. It is more difficult to remember how to say the letters when they are not organized by sound.

Let students practise saying the alphabet aloud in pairs, then point to letters at random and elicit them from the students. Pay special attention to the vowels as these often give problems.

d First put some known words on the board and elicit the spelling. (You could feed in *Can you spell it, please?* at this point.)

Then put students in pairs to practise spelling the words in the book. Go over the answers with the class.

Additional ideas

Here are two spelling games that you can play: Hangman and Anagrams. You can use these at the beginning or end of lessons as warmers or fillers to revise vocabulary.

Hangman You can divide students into two or three teams for this, or play as a class.

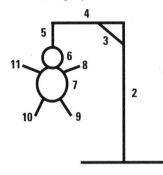

Choose a word and indicate on the board the number of letters it has, using a dash for each letter (i.e. if your word is *doctor*, write _ _ _ _ _ _). One team/The class suggests a letter. If the letter appears in your word, write it in the right place on the dashes, as many times as it appears (i.e. if the letter suggested is *o*, you should write _ o _ _ o _ for the word *doctor*). If the letter doesn't appear in your word, write the letter in that team's column at the side of the board with a line through it, and draw one line of the gallows. Then the second team suggests a letter, and so on.

If you are playing in teams, the winning team is the one that guesses the final letter to complete the word or that guesses the whole word at an earlier point. If you complete the drawing of the gallows before the teams/the class guess the word, then you win and the teams/class lose.

Anagrams Write the jumbled letters of a word on the board. Ask students to unjumble the letters and work out the word in pairs or teams.

GRAMMAR SUMMARY

This is a whole-class activity. Read through the substitution tables with the students. You may like to have students close their books, and you write the tables on the board. You could leave gaps and elicit the answers for some of the substitution items, e.g. for 1 or 2 you could write up *his* but elicit *her*.

Draw students' attention to the full and contracted forms of the verb *to be*. Then either do the **Exercise** as a class, with students suggesting answers for the gaps, or have students work in pairs and then check answers with the whole class.

Word List

Ask the students to turn to page 75 and go through the words with them. Ask them to learn the words for homework, and test them on a few in the following lesson.

Additional material

Workbook Unit 2

Exercises 6 and 7 These provide further practice of *Where … from?* and revision of questions and answers from Unit 1.

Exercise 9 Short forms.

Exercise 10 In this exercise students translate sentences containing the main grammar points presented in the unit.

UNIT 2 TAPESCRIPTS

Tapescript 10

A What's his name?	A What's her name?
B His name's Luc.	B Her name's Ann.

Tapescript 11

the United States	Spain	France
England	Italy	Japan

Tapescript 12

María Where are you from?
Carlo I'm from Italy. Where are you from?
María I'm from Spain.

Tapescript 13

A Where's Ann from?	A Where's Luc from?
B She's from England.	B He's from France.

Tapescript 14

A Hello. What's your name?
B My name's Lídia.
A Where are you from, Lídia?
B I'm from Spain.

Tapescript 15

a h j k	f l m n s x z	q u w
b c d e g p t v	i y	r
	o	

UNIT 3

Jobs – Personal details – Questions and negatives – Numbers 21–100

Introduction to the Unit

This unit introduces some jobs, along with some basic questions. Negatives and short answers in the first and third persons are dealt with for the first time. Students are also introduced to the idea of word stress, and are given their first fairly long unseen listening. Numbers 21–100 are introduced.

Notes on the Unit

PRESENTATION

This presentation practises the question *What's his/her job?* and introduces some job vocabulary. Students will already be familiar with *doctor* and *teacher* from the Reading in Unit 2, so you can concentrate on the question.

1a **T 16** Students look at the photos and either read and listen or just listen to the questions and answers. Then they listen and repeat, after you or the cassette. Concentrate on pronunciation and intonation, and practise the questions and answers in open and closed pairs.

⚠️ Point out the caution box to the students. It draws attention to the fact that we use an article before jobs. You may like to write the sentences up on the board and circle the *a*'s.

b If you think students might know some of the jobs, put them in pairs or threes and ask them to match any jobs they know and guess the others. Then check answers with the class. If you think students won't have any of the vocabulary or won't want to hazard guesses in pairs, then do the matching activity as a whole-class exercise.

If you have flash cards of the jobs, so much the better. Hold up a flash card and ask *What's his/her job?* Elicit or tell them the job. Have students repeat the job after you, and then the complete answer, e.g. *Housewife – She's a housewife*. Concentrate on pronunciation.

Once the exercise is completed, hold up a job flash card or point to one of the pictures in the book at random in order to check students' memories. If you are using flash cards, you could hand them round one to each student and students could then ask each other *What's his/her job?*

Answers			
a teacher	1	a taxi driver	5
a housewife	6	a doctor	3
a shop assistant	8	a policeman	7
a travel agent	4		

c Students ask and answer about the pictures in the book in pairs.

2a This exercise presents third-person personal information questions by means of a simple gap-fill.

Read through Jim's ID card with the class, getting students to repeat *country*, *address*, *phone number*, *age*, *job*, and *student*. Pay attention to word stress. If necessary, explain *student* by pointing to members of the class.

Note that with American addresses, the numbers are said singly, i.e. *one-three-five Broadway*, which avoids the problem of numbers over twenty.

Put students into pairs to fill in the gaps in the questions using the information on the ID card. Note that the word *country* on the card may be new to them. However, they already know the relevant question *Where's he from?* so the second question should not be a problem. The question *How old is he?* is also new and is given in full so that students can familiarize themselves with it before they practise it.

15

b **T 17** Let the students listen to the cassette and check their answers, before you go over the answers with the class.

Before students practise further, model and check the pronunciation of all the questions and answers. Point out that we always give our phone numbers using single figures 0–9.

c In open then closed pairs, students ask and answer about Jim.

> **Additional idea**
>
> For further practice, cut out a picture of a woman from a magazine (or draw one on the board) and provide similar ID information about her. Students then practise asking and answering the questions with *she/her*.

3a/b Yes/No questions and short answers, touched on in **Exercise 2**, are presented here.

T 18 Have students either listen to, or read and listen to, the dialogue a couple of times before they listen and repeat after you or the cassette.

c **T 19** Students have to answer *Yes, he is.* or *No, he isn't.* to questions about Jim on the cassette. Play each question, pause the cassette, and ask students to answer as a class. Alternatively you could turn to the Tapescript and read the questions out yourself.

4a Students are now asked to write Yes/No questions using *she* and different prompts. The ID card provides a number of alternative possibilities about Sonya Bader. Students have to phrase a question about each one.

Read through the ID card and the example with the students. *Hungary* and *Austria* may be new to them, so practise the pronunciation.

In pairs, students write out the questions.

b When students have finished writing, call on individual students to ask you one of the questions they have written. You reply, using this information:

Country	Austria
Age	20
Job	Travel agent
Married	No

Use this opportunity to correct their grammar and pronunciation.

c Students complete the sentences with the information that they have got from you. This exercise practises the negative form in sentences.

d **T 20** Students listen and check their answers. Go over the answers, then practise the sentences as a class.

e **T 21** This is a 'Listen and answer' exercise similar to the one in **3c**, except that here statements are given which the students have to agree with or contradict. As before, pause the cassette after each sentence for students to answer. Alternatively you could turn to the Tapescript and read the sentences out yourself.

5a Yes/No questions in the second person and short answers in the first person are presented here.

T 22 Have students listen to, or read and listen to, the dialogue.

b Go round the class asking Yes/No questions for individual students to answer. Ask about countries, jobs, and marital status as these lend themselves best to this type of question. It may not be appropriate or polite to ask about your students' ages.

Ask plenty of Yes/No questions as students will have to write the questions themselves in the next exercise and it is important that they have fully grasped them.

c In pairs students write their own Yes/No questions. Go round and help them.

> **Answers**
> 2 *Are you* married?
> Other answers will vary.

d Students stand up and go round the class asking one another the questions they wrote in **c**, and answering.

Each student can either interview two or three other students with their full set of questions, or they can mingle more freely putting each question to a different student. Either way, make sure that they get enough practice.

PRACTICE

1 Alone or in pairs, students choose the correct sentence. If students are unsure about number 2, point out that short answers are not contracted. Go over the answers with the class.

> **Answers**
> | 1 | a | ✔ | | 3 | a | ✘ | | 5 | a | ✘ |
> |---|---|---|---|---|---|---|---|---|---|---|
> | | b | ✘ | | | b | ✔ | | | b | ✔ |
> | 2 | a | ✘ | | 4 | a | ✔ | | | | |
> | | b | ✔ | | | b | ✘ | | | | |

2 For this exercise they have to remember the third person questions from the Presentation. See if they can do this without looking back.

Either do the exercise as a class, with individual students asking questions and the whole class writing down the answers, or, if students need more time to think, ask them to write the questions in pairs before putting them to you.

Use these answers, or make up your own:

Name	Isabel Cruz
Country	Brazil
Address	14 Oxford Road, Swindon, England
Phone number	241306
Age	20

Job	Student
Married	Yes

To check the answers, ask individual students the questions and get them to answer. Write the answers on the board. (Non-Europeans in particular may have difficulty with the name and the address, so accept anything that sounds near enough and spell the answers correctly on the board.)

> **Additional material**
> **Workbook Unit 3**
> **Exercise 3** This exercise provides further practice of third person questions.

3a Now students write questions but this time in the second person. They haven't done this before but they should be able to manage it. They can also look back at the third person questions in the Presentation. *How old are you?* has been omitted in case it should cause embarrassment in the speaking activity that follows. However, if you feel that it is appropriate, you can pre-teach it and include it.

> **Answers**
> *Where are* you from?
> *What's your* address?
> *What's your* phone number?
> *What's your* job?
> *Are you* married?

> **Additional material**
> **Workbook Unit 3**
> **Exercise 5** This exercise provides further practice of first person answers.

b Have students copy the grid into their notebooks. Then ask them to stand up and interview their classmates. If you have a monolingual class, students could give their addresses in their own language. Ask students to spell difficult words to each other rather than looking and copying.

c When students have completed three interviews and sat down, ask a few students to report back to the class on another student, thus reverting to the third person forms.

d Students write about another student in their class while you monitor. Afterwards the written work can be passed around the class and read.

PRONUNCIATION

In this section, students are introduced to word stress. This may be an unfamiliar concept if their native language is not stress-timed, but syllable-timed (e.g. Spanish or Japanese).

Students will have to identify the number of syllables in a word, so they are given examples of one-, two-, and three-syllable words.

1a `T 23` Students listen to the pronunciation and read the words. Then they practise saying the words themselves with you. Exaggerate the stress at first so that students hear it clearly.

b In pairs, students do the exercise, saying the words to themselves and putting them in the correct column. *Married* may cause problems as it looks as if it has three syllables.

c `T 24` Let students listen and check their own answers before you go over them with the class.

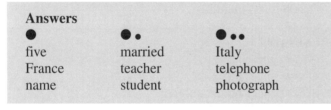

Answers		
●	●.	●..
five	married	Italy
France	teacher	telephone
name	student	photograph

LISTENING

This is the first fairly long unseen listening, so be prepared to play the recording as many times as necessary and to give the students plenty of support and encouragement however well or poorly they do. Unseen listenings of any significant length are always nerve-racking when encountered for the first time at this level. Tell the students that this activity gets much easier with practice.

1a Read through the form with the students.

b/c `T 25` The first time you play the recording, ask the students only to listen, not to write. They will then pick up a little and get the general idea. After listening, ask students to work in pairs and pool what they can remember, and then try to fill in some of the information on the form.

Let them listen a second time, again without writing. In pairs, they can try to fill in more information.

After listening a third time, they can complete the remaining gaps before you go over the answers with the class. (If students want to hear the conversation a

fourth or fifth time before you give them the answers, allow them to. If they are having real difficulties, you can always tell them to turn to the Tapescript on page 71 of the Student's Book and read the text.)

Answers	
Age	*18*
Job	*Student*
Married	*No*
Country	*Scotland*
Address	*10, Links Road, Peebles.*
Phone number	*477 8924*

EVERYDAY ENGLISH

Numbers 21–100

This is the first introduction to numbers over 20. You will have to come back to them and practise them further, but students can familiarize themselves with them now.

1a `T 26` Let students read and listen to the numbers once or even twice. Then ask them to listen to, and repeat, each number.

Give the students a minute or two by themselves to practise saying the numbers and to try and learn them.

Then you can write random numbers (in figures) on the board for them to say.

b `T 27` This exercise helps students to distinguish between the *-teen* and *-ty* endings, which cause problems, not least because the stress on *-teen* shifts when the word is in context. However, here, with the numbers spoken in isolation, the stress is:

.●   ●.
thirteen   thirty

so draw students' attention to this. At this point it is not worth explaining that we say

●.
thirteen
in a sentence like *She's thirteen years old.*

Students listen and tick the numbers they hear. Let them compare answers in pairs before they listen a second time (and a third, if necessary). Go over the answers with the class by having individual students say the number they heard with the correct pronunciation.

| **Answers** |
| 13, 40, 50, 16, 70, 18, 19 |

c `T 28` Students listen and write the numbers they hear. They can read answers out to check.

d Students do a number dictation in pairs. Each student writes some numbers between one and a hundred, perhaps ten in all, and then dictates them to their partner. The partner writes down the figures, not the words, and then checks the answers by reading them back. When one student has completed the dictation, they swap roles.

2 This is a further exercise to practise ages in the third person. Students work in pairs to guess and agree on a possible age for the people in the photographs, using English as much as possible. To this end, it may be useful to pre-teach/explain the phrase *I think …*, if you feel this is not over-burdening the students. Here are the characters' actual ages:

Young man	26
Young woman	30
Man	54
Old woman	82
Young boy	8
Young girl	17

Additional material
Workbook Unit 3
Exercises 11 and 12 These provide further practice of numbers.

GRAMMAR SUMMARY

This is a whole-class activity. Read through the substitution tables with the students. You may like to have students close their books, and you write the tables on the board. You could leave gaps and elicit the answers for some of the substitution items.

⚠️ Draw students' attention to the caution box. You may like to write it up on the board. It indicates to students that they cannot contract short answers.

Draw students' attention to the list of full and contracted negative forms, and explain the contracted forms.

Then either do the **Exercise** as a class with students suggesting answers for the gaps, or have students work in pairs and then check answers with the whole class.

Answers
B Yes, I *am*. Where *are* you from?
A I'*m* from England.
B *Is* Ken from England, too?
A No, he *isn't*. He'*s* from Scotland.
B And *are* you married?
A No, I'*m not*, but Ken's married. He'*s* married to Sandra.

Word List
Ask the students to turn to page 75 and go through the words with them. Ask them to learn the words for homework, and test them on a few in the following lesson.

Additional material
Workbook Unit 3
Exercise 1 This exercise provides further practice of *What's his/her job? S/He's a …*
Exercise 2 This is a word puzzle of jobs.
Exercise 4 This provides further practice of third person short answers.
Exercise 6 First, second, and third person questions.
Exercise 7 Matching questions and answers.
Exercise 8 Further practice of the first and third person forms of the verb *to be*.
Exercise 9 Short forms.
Exercise 10 Long forms.
Exercise 13 In this exercise students translate sentences containing the main grammar points presented in the unit.

UNIT 3 TAPESCRIPTS

Tapescript 16

What's his job?   What's her job?
He's a doctor.   She's a teacher.

Tapescript 17

A What's his name?
B Jim Conway.

A Where's he from?
B The United States.
A What's his address?
B 135, Broadway, New York.
A What's his phone number?
B 542 1870.
A How old is he?
B He's nineteen.
A What's his job?
B He's a student.
A Is he married?
B No, he isn't.

Tapescript 18

A Is Jim from the United States?
B Yes, he is.
A Is he a teacher?
B No, he isn't.

Tapescript 19

Is Jim from England?
Is he from the United States?
Is he a policeman?
Is he a shop assistant?
Is he a student?
Is he 17?
Is he 19?
Is he married?

Tapescript 20

Sonya isn't from Hungary. She's from Austria.
She isn't a hairdresser. She's a travel agent.
She isn't 18. She's 20.
She isn't married.

Tapescript 21

Sonya's from England.   She's seventeen.
She's from Austria.   She's twenty.
She's a housewife.   She's married.
She's a doctor.   She's a travel agent.

Tapescript 22

Sonya, are you from Austria?
Yes, I am.

Are you a student?
No, I'm not.

Tapescript 23

Spain	seven	Germany
thanks	England	hamburger
fine	number	hospital

Tapescript 24

five	married	Italy
France	teacher	telephone
name	student	photograph

Tapescript 25

Interviewer	Hello. What's your name, please?
James Gordon	James. James Gordon.
Interviewer	And how old are you, James?
James Gordon	I'm eighteen.
Interviewer	Eighteen. Thank you. Now, are you a student?
James Gordon	Yes. Yes, I am.
Interviewer	And you aren't married, are you?
James Gordon	No, I'm not.
Interviewer	Are you from England, James?
James Gordon	Well, no. I'm from Scotland.
Interviewer	Ah. Scotland. OK, and what's your address in Scotland?
James Gordon	It's 10, Links, L-I-N-K-S Road, Peebles.
Interviewer	Peebles?
James Gordon	Yes. P-E-E-B-L-E-S.
Interviewer	OK. Thank you. And what's your phone number?
James Gordon	It's 477 8924.
Interviewer	That's 477 8924 …
James Gordon	That's right.
Interviewer	Good. Well …

Tapescript 26

twenty-one	twenty-seven	fifty
twenty-two	twenty-eight	sixty
twenty-three	twenty-nine	seventy
twenty-four	thirty	eighty
twenty-five	thirty-one	ninety
twenty-six	forty	a hundred

Tapescript 27

thirteen	fifty	seventy	nineteen
forty	sixteen	eighteen	

Tapescript 28

twenty-one	twenty-five	thirty-two
fifty-seven	forty-three	eighty-six
seventy-eight	ninety-nine	sixty-four
a hundred		

UNIT 4

Family – Possessive 's – Who? – it/they – Classroom language

Introduction to the Unit

This unit introduces the possessive 's with family vocabulary. As it is quite difficult to grasp, the possessive 's comes up again in Unit 6 with objects. *They are* and plural nouns are also introduced here. In the Everyday English section, there is a short introduction to some useful classroom language and some more opportunities for spelling practice.

Notes on the Unit

PRESENTATION

1a Focus students' attention on the photograph and the family tree. Point to one member of the family and ask *Who's this?* to elicit the person's name. Then, in order to further practise *How old is …?* and (*I think*) *She's …*, ask, *How old is Jane?*, etc. to elicit possible ages. The family ages are: 38, 36, 7, and 4 .

b **T 29** You can play the recording, stopping after each sentence for students to choose a word from the box.

Alternatively, if you wish to present and practise the words in the box orally, put the family tree from page 18 of the Student's Book on the board first.

Use this to explain the meanings of the words in the box, e.g. point to Peter and then to Jane and say *Husband. Peter is Jane's husband.* Have students repeat the word in isolation first, then the whole sentence chorally and individually. Make sure they pronounce the possessive 's. Students can then listen to the recording and write the words down as reinforcement.

Answers
2 Peter is Jane's *husband*.
3 Jane is Simon and Katy's *mother*.
4 Peter is Simon and Katy's *father*.
5 Katy is Jane and Peter's *daughter*.
6 Simon is Jane and Peter's *son*.
7 Katy is Simon's *sister*.
8 Simon is Katy's *brother*.
9 Katy and Simon are Jane and Peter's *children*.
10 Jane and Peter are Katy and Simon's *parents*.

c **T 29** Students listen to the recording and repeat (unless they have already done so during the presentation).

d Put the following on the board to explain possessive 's.

Who's Simon?   s = is
He's Katy's brother   s = possessive, not is

If your students speak a non-European language and the word 'possessive' might not be understood, it might help to draw an arrow from Simon back to Katy.

Next, students ask and answer in pairs. Ask *Who's Simon?* yourself first to give them an example.

e **T 30** Students either agree with or contradict and correct the statements they hear on the cassette. Draw their attention to the example speech bubbles in their books, and play the first two statements. Then play the rest, pausing the cassette after each one for students to answer.

Answers
Katy is Simon's sister. *Yes, that's right.*
Peter is Katy's brother. *No, he isn't. Peter is Katy's father.*
Peter is Katy's father. *Yes, that's right.*
Jane is Peter's sister. *No, she isn't. Jane is Peter's wife.*
Jane is Simon's mother. *Yes, that's right.*
Katy is Peter's son. *No, she isn't. Katy is Peter's daughter.*

2a In this exercise students are given further consolidation practice with another, more famous family. Start off the pairwork by doing a few examples with the class first. Then have students work in pairs while you monitor. Check that they are using possessive *'s* correctly.

b In pairs, students guess their ages, too.

> **Answers**
> Their dates of birth:
> Juan Carlos 5.1.38   Sofia 2.11.38   Elena 20.12.63
> Cristina 13.6.65   Felipe 30.1.69

c In pairs, students decide which sentences are true and which are false, and correct the false ones. Demonstrate by doing the first one with a student.

> **Answers**
> 1 ✔
> 2 ✔
> 3 ✘ Felipe is Cristina's brother.
> 4 ✘ Juan Carlos is Cristina's father.
> 5 ✔
> 6 ✘ Felipe is Juan Carlos and Sofia's son.
> 7 ✘ Cristina and Elena are Felipe's sisters.

3a **T31** Students should now be familiar both with family vocabulary and the possessive *'s*. Here, another *-s* ending – plurals – is introduced. *They are* is also introduced for the first time, but this is dealt with more fully in Unit 5.

Let students look at the photos and listen to the cassette once or twice before you ask them to listen and repeat.

> ⚠️ Draw students' attention to the caution box. You may want to write the sentences on the board and circle the plural *-s*. The box points out to the students that adding *-s* makes a word plural, i.e. more than one.

b Either do this exercise as a class, or ask students to work in pairs and then check the answers with the whole class. *Who are ...?* is introduced here. Students complete the last two sentences using the first two as models. Check answers with the class and point out that the possessive *'s* goes on the second name only.

> **Answers**
> A *Who are* Elena, Cristina, and Felipe?
> B *They're* Juan Carlos and Sofia's children.

PRACTICE

1a In pairs, students practise *Who's this? It's ...*, using the photo and the family tree. Go over the answers quickly with the class.

> **Additional material**
> **Workbook Unit 4**
> **Exercises 1 and 2** Further practice of family vocabulary and possessive *'s*.
> **Exercise 4** A short reading providing further practice of family vocabulary and possessive *'s*.
> **Exercises 5 and 6** Further practice of questions with *Who*.

b In pairs, students complete the sentences using the family tree. To check the answers, ask students to read out the questions and answers in open pairs across the class.

> **Answers**
> 2 Who are John's *sons*? Robert and Colin.
> 3 Who's Colin's *mother*? Molly.
> 4 Who's *Robert* and *Colin's* sister? Carolyn.
> 5 Who's *Molly's* husband? John.
> 6 Who's Molly's *daughter*? Carolyn.
> 7 Who are *John* and *Molly's* children? Robert, Colin, and Carolyn.

2 Put students in pairs or groups of three to solve the puzzle.

> **Answer**
> Susan.

3a For further freer practice, it would be ideal if you and your students brought in some family photos. If you have a small enough class, sit them around you and talk about the pictures slowly but naturally and pass them around. Encourage students to ask questions, if possible. Go over the Student's Book examples beforehand.

If you haven't got photos, put your family tree on the board and talk about your family, again quite slowly but naturally. You could then ask a few questions to check understanding, e.g. *Who's this?*, *What's her job?*, etc.

If you don't want to talk about your own family, find a fictitious or a famous family to talk about.

b Put students with photos in pairs or groups of three and get them to ask about each other's pictures. If they don't have photos, they can draw their family trees and ask and answer about them. Go round the class and monitor.

c Ask a few students to choose a photo or someone in a family tree to say a few things about. The person can be from their own or their partner's family.

d This time students write about a family member. Go round helping and checking. The descriptions and the photos can be passed round the class to be read.

4 In pairs, students choose the correct sentence. Go over the answers with the class by asking individual students to read out the correct sentences.

Answers
1	a ✔	3	a ✘	5	a ✔
	b ✘		b ✔		b ✘
2	a ✘	4	a ✘	6	a ✔
	b ✔		b ✔		b ✘

VOCABULARY

Working alone or in pairs, students put the words in the correct columns. Allow them to compare answers with each other before you go over the answers with the class.

Answers

Jobs	Numbers	Countries	Family
hairdresser	two	Germany	son
policeman	seventeen	France	brother
shop assistant	twenty	Italy	mother
travel agent	six	Spain	daughter

READING

a/b Working alone or in pairs, students read the text and answer the questions. You may like to have individual students answer the questions orally first, and then have everyone write down the answers. *Australia* and *their* are new words. *Their* appears in Unit 6, but if students want it explained now, you can put this on the board:

John's daughter → his daughter

Tom and Nicole's daughter → their daughter

You can also put the other possessive pronouns students know on the board, i.e. *my*, *your*, and *her*.

Answers
1 He's from the United States.
2 He's an actor.
3 He's 32.
4 Her name's Nicole Kidman.
5 She's an actress.
6 She's their daughter.
7 She's one year old.

EVERYDAY ENGLISH

Classroom language

This presents some useful English phrases for the classroom, some of which you may already have taught or the students may already have heard you use.

1a/b **T 32** Students read and listen to the dialogue once or twice before repeating it line by line chorally and individually.

c Have students practise reading the dialogue in open pairs for you to check pronunciation and intonation. Then they practise it in closed pairs.

2/3 **T 33** and **T 34** Follow the same procedure as for **1** above.

4 You can have students ask and answer about the pictures of objects in Unit 1 on page 8 (which is good revision), and/or introduce some of the classroom vocabulary which occurs in the Listening in Unit 10, on page 53, e.g. *table, chair, book, video, cassette player, board, picture*.

Ask *What's this in English?* as you go round pointing at the classroom objects. Students can answer *It's …*, or *I don't know.* and ask you to spell/repeat the word. If you want, they can continue this in pairs.

Additional material
Workbook Unit 4
Exercise 14 Further practice of the language in the Everyday English section.

GRAMMAR SUMMARY

This is a whole-class activity. Read through the substitution tables with the students. You may like to have students close their books, and you write the tables on the board. You could leave gaps and elicit the answers for some of the substitution items. Point out the contractions.

Draw students' attention to the caution box. You may want to write the contents up on the board, circling the *'s* in each sentence. It highlights the difference between *'s* for possession and *'s* as a contraction of *is*.

Then either do the **Exercise** as a class, or have students work in pairs and then check the answers with the whole class.

Answers
1 – b   2 – d   3 – a   4 – c

Word List
Ask the students to turn to page 75 and go through the words with them. Ask them to learn the words for homework, and test them on a few in the following lesson.

Additional material
Workbook Unit 4
Exercise 3 Further practice of *They are* and *S/He is*.
Exercise 7 Distinguishing between *'s* for possession and *'s* as a contraction of *is*.
Exercise 8 Vocabulary and possessive *'s*.
Exercise 9 Further practice of *'s* for possession and *'s* as a contraction of *is*, and plural *-s*.
Exercise 10 Vocabulary practice. Find the different word.
Exercise 11 Numbers revision.
Exercise 12 *is* and *are*.
Exercise 13 Word stress. Two-syllable words.
Exercise 15 In this exercise students translate sentences containing the main grammar points presented in the unit.

UNIT 4 TAPESCRIPTS

Tapescript 29

Jane is Peter's wife.
Peter is Jane's husband.
Jane is Simon and Katy's mother.
Peter is Simon and Katy's father.
Katy is Jane and Peter's daughter.
Simon is Jane and Peter's son.
Katy is Simon's sister.
Simon is Katy's brother.
Katy and Simon are Jane and Peter's children.
Jane and Peter are Katy and Simon's parents.

Tapescript 30

Simon is Peter's son.
Katy is Simon's mother.
Katy is Simon's sister.
Peter is Katy's brother.
Peter is Katy's father.
Jane is Peter's sister.
Jane is Simon's mother.
Katy is Peter's son.

Tapescript 31

He's a doctor.
They're doctors.

She's a taxi driver.
They're taxi drivers.

Tapescript 32

A What's this in English?
B It's a notebook.
A Can you spell it, please?
B N-O-T-E-B-O-O-K.
A Thank you.

Tapescript 33

A What's this in English?
B It's a dictionary.
A Sorry. Can you say it again, please?
B A dictionary.

Tapescript 34

A What's this in English?
B Sorry. I don't know.
A Thanks, anyway.

UNIT 5

Food and drink – Present Simple (*I/you/they*) – Short answers – Requests

Introduction to the Unit

This Unit introduces food and drink vocabulary and the Present Simple with *I*, *you*, and *they*. At this point the Present Simple is used with just five verbs: *like*, *eat*, *drink*, *live*, and *work*. Questions with *do* and short answers are also practised. Students are given their second unseen listening. Requests with *Can I have …?* are introduced in the Everyday English section. In the Grammar Summary prepositions are listed in context for the first time.

Notes on the Unit

PRESENTATION

1a In pairs, students match as many words as possible. Tell them to guess if they're not sure. Ask them to compare their answers with another pair.

Tell the students that the words which do not have a corresponding picture in **Exercise 1** are illustrated elsewhere on this double page spread (pages 22–3), so they can try to match these, too.

Go through the vocabulary with the students. If you have flash cards, hold them up and ask *What's this?/What are these?* If not, hold up the book and point to the pictures. Elicit students' answers and drill the words, checking pronunciation.

Answers			
bananas	tea	wine	salad
milk	sandwiches	coffee	oranges

b For further practice, students write the food and drink words in the circles.

T 35 Then they listen and check. In pairs, students can quickly practise saying the words again to themselves.

Answers
Food — pizza, oranges, meat cake, sandwiches, bananas, salad, chocolate, apples, hamburgers
Drink — water, wine, coffee milk, Coke, tea, beer

c Students work in pairs. One student points to a picture anywhere on pages 22–3, and the other student says the word. Demonstrate the exercise with a good student first.

2a **T 36** Focus students' attention on the pictures. Play the cassette once or twice before you ask them to repeat.

b Students fill in the gaps with *like* and *don't like*. This is the first time that they will have seen Present Simple positive and negative, so put them on the board. Also put up *do not* and show them the contraction *don't*.

Students may ask what *do* means. You can explain simply (in the students' own language if possible) that it helps to make questions and negatives (i.e. it is an auxiliary). However, it may be best to teach the question form with *do* as a set phrase for now.

Answers
I like pizza. And I *like* cake.
I don't like salad. And I *don't like* apples.

c **T 37** Students listen and check their answers.

d Students write down three likes and three dislikes of their own in full sentences. Then in pairs, students tell their partners what they have written and compare their likes and dislikes. Ask a few students to read their lists out to the class.

e **T 38** The question form *Do you like…?* is introduced here. Again, it is probably best not to explain the function of *do* at this juncture. Let students listen a

25

couple of times before you ask them to repeat line by line, chorally and individually.

f Go round the class, asking *Do you like ...?* to elicit *Yes, I do.* or *No, I don't.*

g Students ask and answer in pairs, using the words in **1a** above.

⚠️ | Draw students' attention to the caution box. You may like to put it up on the board. It points out the three forms of the Present Simple – the positive, the question, and the negative – highlighting the need for *do* in the question and the negative.

3a **T 39** Here students are introduced to more Present Simple verbs: *live*, *work*, *eat*, and *drink*. Other new words are *vegetarian* and *bookshop*.

Students read the text and listen to the cassette once or twice. Check comprehension of *live* and *work* by making sentences about yourself, e.g. *I live in* (town, country), *I work in* (*this school*), etc. For *eat* and *drink*, point to the relevant circle on page 22. (It is probably not worth going into the fact that *drink* is a verb here but a noun on page 22.) You should be able to explain *bookshop* with no difficulty and can tell the students that *vegetarian = no meat*.

b **T 40** Students read and listen to the questions once or twice.

Answers
1 Yes, I do.   4 No, I don't.
2 Yes, I do.   5 No, I don't.
3 Yes, I do.

c **T 41** Either have students look back at the reading to find the answers and then write *Yes, I do.* or *No, I don't.*, or, if students are struggling, play **T 41** first to allow them to hear the questions and answers before they write.

Play the cassette for students to check their answers, then go over the answers with the class.

d Before putting students into pairs, demonstrate by asking individual students the questions from **b** above. Ask a few more for variety, e.g. *Do you live in London?*, *Do you work in a hospital?*, etc.

In pairs, students continue asking and answering. Go round and monitor.

4a This text includes *they*, which students encountered briefly in Unit 4. The exercise demonstrates that the

third person plural form of the Present Simple is the same as the first and second person forms.

Students read the text and fill in the gaps with verbs.

Answers
Joe and Barbara *live* in Birmingham.
They *work* for Cadbury's.
They *like* music and tennis.
They *don't like* chocolate.

b Students write Yes/No questions with *they*, using the prompts. Again, this exercise shows them that the verb pattern for questions is the same as the pattern for the second person which they practised in **Exercise 3b**.

Answers
1 Do they live in London? *No they don't.*
2 Do they live in Birmingham? *Yes, they do.*
3 Do they work for IBM? *No, they don't.*
4 Do they work for Cadbury's? *Yes, they do.*
5 Do they like tennis? *Yes, they do.*
6 Do they eat chocolate? *No, they don't.*

c/d In pairs, students ask and answer the questions about Joe and Barbara. Make sure they read the speech bubbles first and use them as examples. They should refer to the text in **4a** for the answers. They should do this exercise orally first, and then write the answers for further practice.

PRACTICE

1a Students work in pairs to complete the puzzle. Go over the answers with the class.

Answers

S	A	N	**D**	W	I	**C**	H	E	S
	O		**R**	A	N	G	E	S	
	P		**I**	Z	Z	A	S		
B	A	N	**A**	N	A	S			
C	O		**K**	E					

b In pairs, students make simple food and drink puzzles themselves. These can be individual words – they do not have to be linked vertically like the puzzle in the Student's Book. Put a couple of examples on the board first, e.g. *W _ _ E* (wine), *_ _ T _ R* (water). When pairs have devised their puzzles, they swap with another pair and try to solve theirs.

Alternatively, play Hangman or Anagrams with food and drink vocabulary. The instructions for this game can be found on page 14.

2 In pairs, students choose the correct sentence. Go over the answers by asking individual students to read out the correct sentence to the class.

Answers
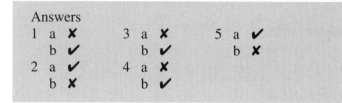

1 a ✗
   b ✔
2 a ✔
   b ✗
3 a ✗
   b ✔
4 a ✗
   b ✔
5 a ✔
   b ✗

3a Individual students interview you and complete the first column of the questionnaire. Check question formation and pronunciation.

b Students stand up and interview three other students.

4a In pairs, students write questions using the substitution tables.

Possible answers
Do they like …
wine / football / coffee / tennis / beer?
Do they work …
in Rome / in a factory / in Paris / in a bank?
Do they drink …
wine / coffee / beer?
Do they live …
in Rome / in Paris?

b Students change partners and ask and answer the questions they have written. They use the pictures to answer.

Possible answers
Do they like pop music? Yes, they do.
Do they like wine? Yes, they do.
Do they like football? Yes, they do.
Do they live in Rome? No, they don't.
Do they work in a factory? No, they don't.
Do they drink coffee? Yes, they do.
Do they live in Paris? Yes, they do.
Do they work in a bank? Yes, they do.
Do they like tennis? No, they don't.
Do they drink beer? No, they don't.

LISTENING AND SPEAKING

This is a fairly long, though fairly simple, unseen listening. You could set the scene by drawing two people at a party on the board, or by using a picture from a magazine. If not, at least write the two names Martin and Isabel on the board.

1a **T 42** Students listen to the conversation once or twice.

b **T 42** Focus students' attention on the choice of answers for Martin. Read through the alternatives with the students but do not elicit answers yet.

You could put students in pairs to choose the correct answers before playing the cassette again. Go over the answers by playing the conversation again and pausing the cassette after each correct answer.

Answers
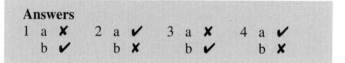

1 a ✗   2 a ✔   3 a ✗   4 a ✔
   b ✔   b ✗   b ✔   b ✗

c Turn to the Tapescript and have students read the conversation in pairs.

Then ask students to work in pairs and, ideally with their books closed, to make similar conversations about themselves. This is their first real role-play so don't expect too much! If some pairs do well, you could ask them to act it out in front of the class.

EVERYDAY ENGLISH

Requests

This is a simple dialogue in a snack bar for the students to learn by heart. *Can I have …?* is new, and can be taught as a set phrase. If you can translate it idiomatically, then do so, otherwise the sense should be fairly clear from the context.

1a/b **T 43** Students look at the photograph and then read and listen to the dialogue once or twice before repeating each line chorally and individually.

c Have students practise the dialogue first in open then in closed pairs.

d In closed pairs, students continue practising the dialogue, choosing alternatives from the box and taking it in turns to make requests. Go round and monitor.

GRAMMAR SUMMARY

This is a whole-class activity. Read through the substitution tables with the students. You may like to have students close their books, and you write the tables on the board. You could leave gaps and elicit the answers for some of the substitution items.

Draw students' attention to the contractions and the short answers.

The prepositions are given in context here and in subsequent units. Students often have a great deal of difficulty with prepositions so you should tell the students to learn them by heart. You can test them now and in the following lesson by putting the sentences on the board with gaps and having students put in the prepositions. Then either do the **Exercise** as a class, with students suggesting answers, or have students work in pairs and then check answers with the whole class.

Answers
1–c   2–a   3–b   4–d

Word List
Ask the students to turn to page 75 and go through the words with them. Ask them to learn the words for homework, and test them on a few in the following lesson.

Additional material

Workbook Unit 5
Exercise 3 Present Simple with *I* and five verbs.
Exercise 6 *is*, *are*, or *do*.
Exercise 10 *is* or *are*.
Exercise 11 Matching questions with answers.
Exercise 13 In this exercise students translate sentences containing the main grammar points presented in the unit.

UNIT 5 TAPESCRIPTS

Tapescript 35

Food

cake	meat	bananas	hamburgers
pizza	chocolate	salad	
oranges	sandwiches	apples	

Drink

| coffee | wine | milk | beer |
| water | tea | Coke | |

Tapescript 36

I like beer.   I don't like water.

Tapescript 37

I like pizza.   I don't like salad
And I like cake.   And I don't like apples.

Tapescript 38

A Do you like pizza?   A Do you like salad?
B Yes, I do.   B No, I don't.

Tapescript 39

Hi! I'm Susan. I live in Glasgow in Scotland. I work in a bookshop. I like my job. I like the weekends, too! I don't eat meat. I'm a vegetarian. I don't drink coffee. I don't like it.

Tapescript 40

1 Do you live in Glasgow?   4 Do you eat meat?
2 Do you work in a bookshop?   5 Do you drink coffee?
3 Do you like your job?

Tapescript 41

1 Do you live in Glasgow?
   Yes, I do.
2 Do you work in a bookshop?
   Yes, I do.
3 Do you like your job?
   Yes, I do.
4 Do you eat meat?
   No, I don't.
5 Do you drink coffee?
   No, I don't.

Tapescript 42

Isabel	Hello. What's your name?
Martin	Martin Hobbs. And what's your name?
Isabel	Isabel Oliveira. Do you live here in London?
Martin	I work in London, but I live in Reading.
Isabel	What's your job?
Martin	I'm a travel agent. And you?
Isabel	I'm a doctor.
Martin	Where are you from, Isabel?
Isabel	Portugal.
Martin	Oh, I like Portugal.
Isabel	Really?
Martin	Oh, yes. Very much. I like the food and the wine, especially.
Isabel	Oh, yes. What about the weather …?

Tapescript 43

A Good afternoon. Can I have a coffee, please?
B Certainly... Here you are.
A Thank you very much.

Objects and adjectives – *a/an* – *have* – *their* – *Is this your …?* – Days of the week

Introduction to the Unit

This unit introduces adjectives and objects with the indefinite article *a/an*, and the verb *have*. *Is this your …?* and the possessive *'s* are also practised with objects and belongings. The Everyday English section introduces days of the week and times of the day with the question word *When*.

Notes on the Unit

PRESENTATION

1a In pairs, students match as many of the pictures as possible. They should know *dictionary* and *notebook* already. If they are struggling, do the activity as a class.

Once the meaning of the new words has been established, drill them chorally and individually.

Answers		
1 key	2 ticket	3 postcard
4 magazine	5 dictionary	6 map
7 bag	8 stamp	9 notebook

b Students ask and answer about the objects. If you want to make the exercise more difficult, tell them to cover the word written below it when they point to a picture.

2a You could ask students *What are these letters?* (Answer: vowels). Ask students to say the vowels. European students should be able to answer, at least in their own language. If students speak a language like Japanese or Arabic, the concept of vowels may be foreign to them. In this case, it may be best simply to have them learn the rule governing the use of *a* and *an*.

b You may wish to do this exercise as a class. Students should be able to fill in *apple* in number 2 (it appeared in Unit 5), then all they have to do is work out the rule and volunteer *an* for numbers 3 and 4.

Answers
2 It's an *apple*.
3 It's *an* envelope.
4 It's *an* umbrella.

c Students write *a* or *an* before the nouns. Most of these nouns have come up in previous units, but even if students can't remember the meanings, they should be able to complete the exercise satisfactorily.

When students have finished, go over the answers and drill pronunciation. Make sure students say,

a h̲ospital   an a̲ctor   an o̲ffice   etc.

Answers	
a hospital	*an* exercise
a television	*a* question
an actor	*an* answer
an office	*a* cassette
an assistant	*an* address

3 On page 65 of the Teacher's Book there are some simple flash cards of objects from the first six units. Make one photocopy of the objects for each pair, and give eight objects to each student.

Model the activity with a student, holding up a card and eliciting *It's a/an …* Then have students close their books and ask and answer in the same way about the objects.

4a **T 44** This is the first presentation of the verb *have*. Play the dialogue once or twice for students to listen and read, or just to listen.

b **T 44** Play the cassette again, pausing after each line to drill it chorally and individually. Make sure students say /dʒʊ/ or /dʒuː/ for *Do you …?*

c Students complete the sentences using **4a** as a model.

d **T 45** Students listen and check their answers. Then drill the dialogue, line by line.

Answers
A *Do* you *have* a video?
B Yes, I *do*.
A *Do* you *have* a computer, too?
B No, I *don't*.

e In pairs, students ask about each other's families and possessions and give true answers.

5a Students write the numbers of the relevant pictures in the boxes next to the adjectives. This can be done in pairs or, if students are having difficulty, as a class. When you check the answers, drill pronunciation at the same time.

Additional idea
As a follow-up you can play a card game with the flash cards from **Exercise 3** and these lists:

S1	S2	S3	S4
map	envelope	ticket	pen
key	postcard	magazine	apple
address	notebook	umbrella	dictionary
bag	stamp	orange	office

Put the students into groups of four and deal out four cards to each student. (Students can play in groups of three if you remove one list and the four objects on the cards.)

Give each student a list of items to collect. They should not show the list to the other members of the group.

Students take it in turns to ask for an object that they need from one of the other students in the group, e.g.

Marie, do you have a key?
Yes, I do.
Can I have it, please?

The first person to collect all four items on their list is the winner.

Answers
2 old 5 expensive 6 cheap
4 small 1 new 3 big

b Working alone or in pairs, students write the answers below the pictures. They can check answers with another student or pair. Go over the answers, making sure that they don't use *an* before *apple* this time (because it is *a big apple*) but that they do use it before *expensive* in *an expensive bag*. Explain that in English the adjective comes before the noun. This is especially important if it is different in their own language.

Answers
3 a big apple
4 a small apple
5 an expensive bag
6 a cheap bag

6a Have students read the postcard silently first, then ask individual students to read a sentence aloud each. *Beautiful* and *interesting* will probably be new to the students. Give translations if you can, or put the words into simple sentences, e.g. (famous person) *is beautiful.*, *I like this book. It's interesting.*

b Students find the possessive adjectives in the text and complete the table.

Answers
I	my
you	*your*
he	*his*
she	her
they	*their*

PRACTICE

1a Students put some of their objects and belongings on the desk in front of them, and ask each other questions. Feed in new vocabulary where necessary.

b Collect some of the students' objects, one from each person. Redistribute them to different students. Students then stand up and go round the class with the object you have given them, asking *Is this your …?*

Additional idea
In order to revise the possessive *'s* with objects, you could collect all the objects again and put them on a desk. Then ask, for example, *Manuel, is this Louisa's pencil?* Have students ask similar questions in open pairs across the room until all the objects have been identified and delivered back to their owners.

2 Working in pairs or alone, students do the writing exercise as a follow-up. Go over the answers with the class.

Answers
1 It's *her* key.
2 Is it *his* bag?
3 It's *their* house.
4 It's *his* newspaper.
5 Is this *their* hotel?
6 It's *her* dictionary.

3 Students make true sentences with the adjectives in the box. You will have to explain *friendly*. (This word comes up again in the reading on Dublin on page 22 of the Workbook.)

4 Working alone or in pairs, students choose the odd sentence out. Each odd sentence contains a different grammatical construction from the other three sentences.

Students compare answers with another student or pair. Go over the answers with the class.

Answers
1 c	2 d	3 b	4 c

5 In this exercise students practise *Do you have …?* by means of a questionnaire.

a Students fill in the first column for themselves.

b Then have individual students ask you the questions. Check their grammar and pronunciation. The students complete the second column as they hear your answers.

c This is a 'mingle' activity. Students stand up and ask three other students the questions and fill in their charts. Note that they cannot report back their findings

to you unless you feed in third person *has* (which is not introduced formally until Unit 8). You may wish to do this as *has* appears passively in the reading on Dublin on page 22 of the Workbook.

READING AND WRITING

1a Working alone or in pairs, students choose either New York or Prague, then read the postcard and choose adjectives to complete the text. You may need to explain *weather*. Ask three or four students to read out their postcards. The other students listen and see if their postcards are the same or different.

b In pairs or alone, students write a postcard of their own. You can use this opportunity to feed in extra vocabulary, for example, you could teach them *The people are friendly*. If the students are up to it, encourage them to experiment with their English, and help them with words like *shops* and *buildings*, etc.

EVERYDAY ENGLISH

Days of the week

1a **T 46** Students listen to and repeat the days of the week. Drill pronunciation, then go round the class with each student saying one day of the week in the correct order.

b Students translate the days of the week into their own language.

c Students do the exercise in pairs. They can ask and answer orally or they can write the answers.

2 Here students learn which prepositions are used with the days of the week and the times of the day. They need to know these for Unit 7.

T 47 Students listen and repeat.

!

Draw students' attention to the caution box. You may like to put it up on the board, circling the two prepositions. It points out the difference between *in the evening* but *on Saturday evening*, *in the afternoon* but *on Friday afternoon*, etc.

3a **T 48** This dialogue introduces questions with *When* and practises the use of prepositions with days and times. Point out that the plural isn't used with *from Monday to Friday*, but it is used with *on Tuesday and Thursday evenings* (meaning generally *every Tuesday or Thursday*). Play the dialogue once or twice for the students to listen and read.

b **T 48** Play the cassette again, pausing after each line to drill it chorally and individually.

c In closed pairs, students ask and answer the three questions about themselves. If your students don't have jobs, ask them to use *go to school* or *college* instead of *work* in the first question. And if students don't drink coffee, make sure they answer *I don't drink coffee*!

Additional material

Workbook Unit 6
Exercise 10 Days of the week.

GRAMMAR SUMMARY

This is a whole-class activity. Read through the substitution tables with the students. You may like to have students close their books, and you write the tables on the board. You could leave gaps and elicit the answers for some of the substitution items.

!

Draw students' attention to the two caution boxes. You may like to put them up on the board. The first indicates to students that they cannot contract short answers. The second reminds them to use *an* before any word beginning with a vowel.

Then either do the **Exercise** as a class, with students suggesting corrections, or have students work in pairs and then check answers with the whole class.

Answers
1 This is *an* orange.
2 *Do you have* a dictionary?.
3 I *don't* know.
4 Is this a map? Yes, *it is*.

Word List
Ask the students to turn to page 76 and go through the words with them. Ask them to learn the words for homework, and test them on a few in the following lesson.

Additional material

Workbook Unit 6
Exercise 9 General revision.
Exercise 11 In this exercise students translate sentences containing the main grammar points presented in the unit.
Exercise 12 A crossword.

UNIT 6 TAPESCRIPTS

Tapescript 44

A Do you have a brother?
B Yes, I do. Three brothers!
A Do you have a sister, too?
B No, I don't.

Tapescript 45

A Do you have a video?
B Yes, I do.
A Do you have a computer, too?
B No, I don't.

Tapescript 46

Monday	Thursday	Saturday
Tuesday	Friday	Sunday
Wednesday		

Tapescript 47

in the morning	on Sunday
in the afternoon	on Monday morning
in the evening	on Friday afternoon
on Monday	on Sunday evening
on Friday	at weekends

Tapescript 48

A When do you work?
B From Monday to Friday.
A When do you have English lessons?
B On Tuesday and Thursday evenings.
A When do you drink coffee?
B In the mornings and evenings.

STOP AND CHECK 1 UNITS 1-6

This Stop and Check section allows students to revise what they have learnt so far. It can be used in a number of ways.

- You can set it in class as an informal progress test, and take in their work to correct.
- You can put students in groups to work on the exercises. They can then score their own or another student's answers as you go over the answers with the class.
- You can give the written parts for homework. Students can go over their answers in small groups in the next lesson, before doing the listening and speaking exercises with you in class.

It can be very productive for students to work in groups and try to persuade their peers of the right answer. Many previous lessons are recalled. It also takes the stress out of a 'test' situation, and with all the group discussion everyone should have a reasonably high score!

n.b. Turn to page 66 for the photocopiable speaking activity in Exercise 7, page 31. Point out to students that a male and a female name are given in each case and they should choose whichever is appropriate for them.

STOP AND CHECK 1

Tapescript 49

Interviewer	Mr Green, do you like music?
Simon Green	Oh, yes, I do. Very much.
Interviewer	Do you have a radio?
Simon Green	Yes, I do.
Interviewer	And do you have a CD player?
Simon Green	No, I don't.
Interviewer	Miss Taylor, do you like music?
Pauline Taylor	No, I don't. Not very much.
Interviewer	Oh, dear! Well, do you have a radio?
Pauline Taylor	Yes, I do.
Interviewer	And do you have a CD player?
Pauline Taylor	No, I don't. They're very expensive.
Interviewer	Mr Patel, do you like music?
Atish Patel	Yes, I do. Yes.
Interviewer	Oh, well, do you have a radio?
Atish Patel	Yes, of course.
Interviewer	Do you have a CD player, too?
Atish Patel	Yes, I do.

Tapescript 50

interesting	bananas	magazine
envelope	computer	afternoon
beautiful	expensive	
newspaper	policeman	
hairdresser		
video		

UNIT 7

Activities – *like* + *-ing* – Present Simple negative (*I/you/we/they*) – Telling the time

Introduction to the Unit

This unit introduces activities with *like* + *-ing*, and further practises the Present Simple with the negative *don't*. Telling the time is introduced and practised in the Everyday English section.

Notes on the Unit

PRESENTATION

1a In pairs, students match the activity words and phrases with the pictures as best they can. Encourage them to guess ones they don't know. Go over the answers with the class, drilling pronunciation at the same time.

> **Answers**
> (Clockwise from top)
> listening to music   watching television
> singing   swimming
> cooking   dancing
> playing tennis   reading
> going out with friends eating in restaurants

b Students work in pairs while you monitor. One student points to a picture of an activity, the other says what it is.

> **Additional idea**
> You could continue with a whole-class extension if the students are not averse to miming. Ask individual students to mime one of the activities for others to guess.

2a **T 51** Students read and listen to the text once or twice before they look at the chart on page 33. You may like to point out *from Tuesday to Saturday* (five consecutive days) again.

b In pairs, students complete the chart. Point out that not every box needs a tick or cross.

Go over the answers by having individual students give you complete sentences based on the information in the chart, e.g. *Lucy and Nicole like swimming.* Check grammar and pronunciation.

Answers	Mr Johnson	Mrs Johnson	Polly	Lucy	Nicole
swimming	☐	☐	✗	✓	✓
watching television	✓	✓	✓	✓	✓
listening to music	✗	✗	✗	✓	✓
reading	✓	✓	✓	☐	☐
cooking	✓	✓	✗	✗	✗
going out with friends	☐	☐	✓	✓	✓

3 This exercise practises *like* + gerund, e.g. *I like playing tennis*, and contrasts it with the Present Simple with *when* where the verb is in the infinitive form, e.g. *When do you play tennis?* Point out that we say *When do you go swimming?* not *When do you swim?*

a/b **T 52** Students read and listen (or just listen) to the conversation once or twice. Then students fill in the gaps. This can be done either in closed pairs, or as whole-class activity on the board.

> ⚠️ Draw students' attention to the caution box. You may like to put it up on the board. It draws attention to the gerund after *like*.

T 52 Students listen and check once more. Go over the answers with the class by having individual students read out a completed line of the dialogue each.

You may wish to spend a little more time on pronunciation and intonation before moving on to the closed pair practice in **c**.

Answers
Mike   Do you and your sisters like *swimming*, Polly?
Polly   I don't, but Lucy and Nicole do. I like *playing* tennis. Do you like *swimming*, Mike?
Mike   Yes, I do. Very much. But I don't like *playing* tennis! When do you *play* tennis?
Polly   On Sundays or Mondays. When do you *go* swimming?
Mike   On Saturday afternoons.
Polly   Oh, Lucy and Nicole *go* swimming then, too.

c Students practise the dialogue in closed pairs while you monitor.

PRACTICE

1a Students look at the questionnaire and complete the first column about themselves.

b Before getting students to fill in the rest of the chart, demonstrate by having two students ask and answer a couple of questions in open pairs. Students then work with a partner in closed pairs and ask and answer questions to complete the chart.

c Now students have to find out when their partner does the activities he/she likes doing. Point out that they must be careful not to use the gerund now for the main verb, but that it appears in the phrases *go swimming* and *go dancing*.

d Choose two or three pairs of students to compare their likes and dislikes and report back to the class, using *We*. Feed in the word *both*.

e Put the pairs of students in groups of four and have them compare their answers again. They should try to find something they all like or don't like. Feed in the word *all*.

Ask one or two groups to report back to the class.

2 Students work in closed pairs to read the information in the chart and then use it to complete the text below. You might need to fill in the first one or two gaps with

the whole class to make sure they have understood the task.

Go over the answers by having individual students round the class read out sentences from the completed text.

Answers
Hello. Our names are Paula and Marco Branco. We're from Brazil. Our father's a sports teacher and our mother's a primary school teacher. They work from Monday to Friday. We *don't* work. We're students. We *go* to school from Monday to Saturday. In the evenings we all *like* watching television and listening to music. Marco and I *like* singing. We sing in a band at school. Our parents *don't like* singing. They like dancing. They go dancing on Thursday evenings. At weekends Marco and I *like* going out with our friends. On Sundays we all *go* to church.

Additional material
Workbook Unit 7
Exercises 1 and 2 Further practice of activities and *like*.
Exercise 12 Reading texts on likes and dislikes.

---

3 Working alone or in pairs, students make the sentences negative. Go over the answers with the class.

Answers
1 You don't like Tina Turner.
2 They don't stay at home on Saturdays.
3 We aren't married.
4 They don't have an old car.
5 He isn't from Italy.

Additional material
Workbook Unit 7
Exercises 3 and 4 Further practice in making negative and positive sentences.

4a Working alone or in pairs, students write the questions.

b **T 53** Allow students to listen to the cassette and check and correct their own answers. Then go over the answers with the class, checking pronunciation and intonation.

Additional material

Workbook Unit 7

Exercise 5 Further practice in making questions with *When*.

c In closed pairs, students ask and answer the questions.

5 Students have to complete the sentences with the correct preposition. Then they choose the affirmative or negative verb and write true sentences about themselves, while you monitor.

Let students compare answers in pairs, then ask each student to read out one sentence.

Additional material

Workbook Unit 7

Exercise 6 Further practice of prepositions.

PRONUNCIATION

This exercise focuses on word stress in two- and three-syllable words.

1a In pairs, students work out the pronunciation of the words and put them in the correct column.

b T 54 Play the cassette for the students to check their answers. Drill any words which caused problems. Draw students' attention in particular to *chocolate* and *evening*, which look as if they have three syllables, but in fact have two.

Then give students a couple of minutes to run through the list, practising saying the words to themselves.

c/d T 55 Repeat the procedure in **a** and **b** above. Draw attention to *dictionary*, which looks as if it has four syllables, but has three.

VOCABULARY

1a This exercise highlights some basic collocations that the students have learnt. Students match words in A and B, working in pairs (or alone and then checking in pairs). Go over the answers with the class.

b Students test each other. One student closes their book, the other student gives a verb and the first has to complete the phrase. Then students change over.

c In closed pairs, students try to think of more phrases to go with each verb. Go over the answers with the class and put the verbs with all the correct collocations on the board.

LISTENING

1a/b **T 56** Students listen and tick or cross the activities. Have students compare their answers in pairs before listening again. Allow students to listen a third time if they want to.

Answers

cooking	✔	watching television	✔
swimming	✘	dancing	✘
reading	✔	eating in restaurants	✔
listening to music	✔		

READING AND WRITING

1a Read through the information about the Crosses with the students. Then ask students to read what Mr and Mrs Cross say in the speech bubble.

In closed pairs, students look at the information about Mr and Mrs Birkan and write what they say, using the Crosses' speech as a model.

Go over the answers with the class by asking some students to read out their versions.

Answer

We're from Turkey and we live in a new house in Istanbul. We have three daughters. We're dentists. We like playing tennis and listening to music.

> **Additional material**
> **Workbook Unit 7**
> **Exercises 7 and 8** Further reading and writing practice.

EVERYDAY ENGLISH

Telling the time

You may like to make a cardboard clock with movable hands for this lesson and for subsequent revision of telling the time.

1a **T 57** Focus attention on the clock. Play the cassette once or twice while students listen and read.

b **T 57** Students repeat the times after you or the cassette.

2a Students write the times, referring to the clocks in **Exercise 1**.

b **T 58** Students listen and check their answers. As you go over the answers, have them practise saying the times.

Answers

It's five o'clock.	It's half past ten.
It's quarter past nine.	It's quarter to four.
It's twenty past seven.	It's ten to eleven.

3a **T 59** Students hear three short conversations. They have to listen for the times and draw them on the clock faces. You may need to pause the cassette after each conversation to give students time to work out and draw in the time.

Students compare their answers with a partner. Allow students to listen to the conversations once or twice more to check their answers, then go over the answers with the class.

Answers

1 Twenty past four.
2 Quarter past eleven.
3 Five to seven.

b If necessary, refer students to the Tapescript at the back of the Student's Book. They can read and practise the conversations in closed pairs for a few minutes.

Then ask them to turn back to the unit and continue practising the conversations, referring only to the clocks. Go round and monitor.

> **Additional material**
> **Workbook Unit 7**
> **Exercises 9 and 10** Further practice in telling the time.

GRAMMAR SUMMARY

This is a whole-class activity. Read through the substitution tables with the students. You may like to have students close their books, and you write the tables on the board. You could leave gaps and elicit the answers for some of the substitution items, e.g. you could write just the main verb or just the auxiliary in tables 4 and 5.

Do the same with the prepositions. Write the sentences on the board with the prepositions missing and ask the class to fill them in. Suggest that students learn them.

Then either do the **Exercise** as a class, or have students work in pairs and then check answers with the class.

Answers

1	a	✗	4	a	✔	7	a	✗
	b	✔		b	✗		b	✔
2	a	✔	5	a	✔			
	b	✗		b	✗			
3	a	✗	6	a	✗			
	b	✔		b	✔			

Word List

Ask the students to turn to page 76 and go through the words with them. Ask them to learn the words for homework, and test them on a few in the following lesson.

Additional material

Workbook Unit 7

Exercise 11 In this exercise students translate sentences containing the main grammar points presented in the unit.

UNIT 7 TAPESCRIPTS

Tapescript 51

Whole family together:
Hello. We're the Johnson family and we live in Leeds.
Polly:
Hello. I'm Polly Johnson. I have two sisters, Lucy and Nicole. My mother, my father, and I are hairdressers. We work from Tuesday to Saturday. We don't work on Sundays and Mondays. My sisters don't work. They are at school. They like swimming on Saturdays. In the evenings we all like watching television. My sisters like listening to music, but my parents and I don't. We like reading. My parents like cooking, but my sisters and I don't! We like going out with our friends at weekends.

Tapescript 52

Mike Do you and your sisters like swimming, Polly?
Polly I don't, but Lucy and Nicole do. I like playing tennis. Do you like swimming, Mike?
Mike Yes, I do. Very much. But I don't like playing tennis! When do you play tennis?
Polly On Sundays or Mondays. When do you go swimming?

Mike On Saturday afternoons.
Polly Oh, Lucy and Nicole go swimming then, too.
Mike Really? Well …

Tapescript 53

1 When do you go to work?
   When do you go to school?
2 When do you drink tea?
3 When do you go to the supermarket?
4 When do you study English at home?
5 When do you go to the cinema?

Tapescript 54

tennis	salad	children	evening
mother	agent	chocolate	actress
Japan	address	cassette	Brazil

Tapescript 55

oranges	factory	Hungary
beautiful	classical	radio
sandwiches	cinema	dictionary
united	assistant	umbrella
computer	policeman	

Tapescript 56

What do I like doing? Let me see. Well, I like cooking, very much. I don't like swimming. I don't like the water! Hmm. Reading. Yes, I like reading very much, and I like listening to music. I like pop music and classical music. Television. Yes, I like watching television in the evenings. But I don't like dancing. No, not at all! And yes, I like eating in restaurants very much. I sometimes eat in restaurants at weekends.

Tapescript 57

It's two o'clock.	It's half past two.
It's quarter past two.	It's quarter to three.
It's twenty past two.	It's ten to three.

Tapescript 58

It's five o'clock.	It's half past ten.
It's quarter past nine.	It's quarter to four.
It's twenty past seven.	It's ten to eleven.

Tapescript 59

1 A Oh, hello, David. What's the time, please?
   B Um. It's twenty past four.
   A Thanks very much.
2 A Time for a coffee.
   B Why? What's the time?
   A It's quarter past eleven.
   B Oh, good.
3 A Hurry up. We're late.
   B What's the time?
   A It's five to seven.
   B Oh, OK.

Present Simple (*he/she/it*) – Short answers – Social English 1

Introduction to the Unit

This unit provides an introduction to Present Simple verbs in the third person and in short answers. In the Everyday English section students practise the difference between *Excuse me* and *Sorry*.

Notes on the Unit

PRESENTATION

1a **T 60** Students look at the picture, and read and listen to the text. (Alternatively, you could ask students to cover the text and just listen. Then they can listen a second time with the text uncovered.)

b Students use the information in the text to complete the sentences.

c **T 61** Students listen and check their answers before you ask them what the last letter of the verbs is.

> **Answers**
> Rita *works* in a hospital.
> She *arrives* at the hospital at nine o'clock.
> She *likes* her job.

Put the eight subject pronouns (*I*, *you*, *he*, etc.) on the board and elicit or feed in the correct forms of the verb *work*. The completed table will look like this:

I	work	We	work
You	work	You	work
He	work<u>s</u>	They	work
She	work<u>s</u>		
It	work<u>s</u>		

Highlight the *-s* in the third person. This is the first time that they will have seen the Present Simple fully conjugated.

2a If possible, translate *usually*, *sometimes*, and *never* into the students' own language. If not, write the following on the board:

I don't like coffee. I **never** drink coffee.   0%
I **sometimes** go out with friends on Friday
evenings.   40%
I **usually** get up at 7 o'clock on Mondays.   90%

Although *usually* is not strictly the same as the other adverbs of frequency, this explanation will suffice for now. These words come up again in Unit 12, along with other adverbs of frequency, where they are given more practice, so treat them as items of vocabulary for the moment.

b In closed pairs, students complete the text with the verbs. Go over the answers by having individual students read out a sentence each.

> **Answers**
> Michael Riley is from Ireland, but he *lives* in Cambridge. He isn't married. He's a journalist and he *works* at home from Monday to Thursday. On Fridays he *works* in London. He has a car and he *drives* to London. At weekends he usually *plays* tennis and *cooks* dinner for his friends.

3a/b **T 62** Students correct the sentences, then listen and check their answers. It is to be hoped that they will notice the difference in spelling between *lives/eats* and *goes*. Write ~~gos~~ on the board.

> **Answers**
> 1 He live*s* in Oxford.
> 2 She sometimes eat*s* in a restaurant.
> 3 She go*es* to the centre of London by train.

4a Write on the board:

Do you live in London?
Do<u>es</u> Rita live in London?

Highlight the fact that the spelling rule for *does* is the same as for *goes*. Write ~~dos~~ on the board. Model the pronunciation of *do* /duː/ and *does* /dʌz/.

T 63 Students read and listen to the questions and short answers.

b **T 63** Students repeat after you or the cassette, chorally and individually.

⚠️

> Draw students' attention to the caution box. You may want to put it up on the board, circling the *s* in *does*. It points out that in questions the third person -*s* is added to the auxiliary, not to the main verb. To illustrate this further, you may like to put the following on the board:
>
> She cook⟨s⟩ on Sundays.
>
> Do⟨es⟩ she cook on Sundays?

c Students complete the questions, using **4a** as a model.

d/e **T 64** Students listen, check their answers, and repeat. Make sure they say *Does he live . . .* /dʌziːlɪv/, running the sounds together properly.

Answers
1 *Does* he live in Manchester?
2 *Does* he *work* at home on Fridays?
3 *Does* he *drive* to London?
4 *Does* he *play* football?
5 *Does* he *cook* dinner for his friends?

f Students ask and answer the questions in closed pairs, using the information in the text. Go round and monitor.

Answers
2 *Does* he *work* at home on Fridays? No, he doesn't.
3 *Does* he *drive* to London? Yes, he does.
4 *Does* he *play* football? No, he doesn't.
5 *Does* he *cook* dinner for his friends? Yes, he does.

PRACTICE

1a This is an unseen information gap. Put students in pairs, allotting A and B roles. Ask Bs to turn to page 78. They will see that they have information about Irma but not about Laszlo.

Elicit the first question *Does he play tennis?* from one of the Bs. Tell them to use *he* or *she* in their questions, rather than the names, in order to practise the personal pronouns with *does*. You may also need to draw attention to the fact that there is an -*s* on the verbs in the questionnaire, which they must remember to omit from the main verb in their questions.

Demonstrate by having a student playing a B role ask a question and a student playing an A role answer it. Students then work in closed pairs and ask and answer while you monitor.

Go over the answers with the class by asking random questions, e.g. *Does Laszlo drink beer?*, *Does Irma drive to work?* to elicit *Yes, s/he does.* or *No, s/he doesn't.* from students.

Answers
Laszlo
Does he play tennis? Yes, he does.
Does he read at weekends? No, he doesn't.
Does he drink beer? Yes, he does.
Does he drive to work? Yes, he does.
Does he cook in the evenings? No, he doesn't.
Irma
Does she play tennis? Yes, she does.
Does she read at weekends? Yes, she does.
Does she drink beer? No, she doesn't.
Does she drive to work? No, she doesn't.
Does she cook in the evenings? Yes, she does.

b For further practice, students write sentences about one of the characters. This entails previewing the Present Simple third person negative form. Again, highlight the fact that there is no -*s* on the main verb. If you wish to leave this until it is presented formally in Unit 9, then omit this exercise.

Answers
Laszlo plays tennis. He doesn't read at weekends. He drinks beer. He drives to work. He doesn't cook in the evenings.

Irma plays tennis. She reads at weekends. She doesn't drink beer. She doesn't drive to work. She cooks in the evenings.

Additional material
Workbook Unit 8
Exercise 4 Further practice of third person questions and short answers.

2 In pairs, students complete the questions and short answers. They have to distinguish between first, second, and third person. Go over the answers by having open pairs read out a question and answer, while the rest of the class listens and agrees or disagrees.

Answers
1 *Do* you like red roses?
   Yes, I *do*.
2 *Does* he work for Toyota?
   Yes, he *does*.
3 *Does* she go to the supermarket on Fridays?
   No, she *doesn't*.
4 *Do* they drive to work?
   Yes, they *do*.
5 *Does* he have a CD player?
   No, he *doesn't*.
6 *Do* you learn English on Sundays?
   No, I *don't*.

Additional material
Workbook Unit 8
Exercise 2 Further practice of *do* and *does* to make questions.
Exercise 7 Further practice of *do, does, don't,* and *doesn't*.

3a This is a simple questionnaire to practise Yes/No questions in the second and third person. As a variation, students use *Yes, usually.*, *Yes, sometimes.*, and *No, never.*, which allows them to practise these adverbs in a simple fashion. (In Unit 12 students practise using them in complete sentences.)

To introduce the questionnaire, put the three replies on the board (not omitting the *Yes* or *No* in front). Ask individual students a couple of questions from the questionnaire and elicit the answers.

Students then work in closed pairs, asking and answering, and filling in their partner's answers.

b Students change partners and ask questions in the third person about their new partner's previous partner, and fill in the second table. Go round and monitor.

As a class round-up, ask a few students questions about themselves and then questions about their partners, so that they get practice in switching from first to third person.

4a/b Students read the text and then rewrite it in the third person. Go over the answers by having individual students read out a sentence each. Write the changed verbs and pronouns on the board as you go.

Answers
She's from Salamanca in Spain, but *she lives* in London. *She's* a teacher and *her* husband, Rolando, works for a bank. *She has* one son. He is three. In *her* free time *she likes* swimming and listening to music.

c In closed pairs, students make up sentences about the two people. They can talk about one person each or make up alternate sentences about both people. You may need to give or elicit a couple of example sentences using the speech bubbles as models before students start the pairwork. Go round and monitor.

As class feedback, elicit sentences from individual students.

Answers
Fiona is from Scotland.
She lives in Bristol.
She's a taxi driver.
She's married.
She has a son and two daughters.
She likes listening to music and cooking in her free time.
Shahid is from Pakistan.
He lives in London.
He's a shop assistant.
He isn't married.
He has four sisters and one brother.
He likes reading and playing squash in his free time.

Additional material
Workbook Unit 8
Exercises 1 and 3 Further practice of the Present Simple, third person.

---

5 Students match the questions and answers.

Answers
When does she arrive at work?	At half past eight.
Does he like football?	No, he doesn't.
Is he married?	Yes, he is.
Where does she live?	In Athens.
Does she drink whisky?	No, she doesn't.
What time is it?	It's three o'clock.
Is she a travel agent?	No, she isn't.

6 Working alone or in closed pairs, students write questions and answers using *When* and the information in the chart. Go over the answers by having students ask and answer in open pairs across the class.

Additional material

Workbook Unit 8
Exercise 8 Further practice of third person questions with *When*.

LISTENING

1a/b/c [T 65] Ask students to look at the picture and the box below in pairs and to make notes on where they think Ivor is from, where he lives, what his job is, etc. There are clues to some of the answers in the picture. The students can then listen and check in pairs.

Alternatively, you can do this as a class activity as follows. Put all the students' ideas about Ivor on the board but don't correct them yet. Let students listen to the conversation and compare what they hear with what has been written on the board. Then go through the information on the board, ticking the items that were corroborated by the cassette.

d Allow students to listen once or twice more to check and correct their information.

Answers
From:	Poland
Home:	Oxford, England
Job:	Computer programmer
Married:	Yes
Family:	Wife Kate, and two daughters
Hobbies:	Reading and playing tennis

READING

1a/b Students read the text and write answers to the comprehension questions. They may already be familiar with Eric Cantona. The following language will be new to the students: *play for Manchester United* (= a British football team), *to train*, *to speak*,

philosophy, and *poetry*. If you can't provide a mother tongue translation, then students may need a bilingual dictionary, especially if they are non-European.

(If Eric Cantona is no longer playing for Manchester United or no longer living in England, see if your students can correct any of the information in the text!)

Answers
1 He's from France.
2 He lives in Britain.
3 He's a footballer.
4 Yes, he is.
5 He likes reading philosophy and poetry.

EVERYDAY ENGLISH

Social English 1

These conversations highlight the difference between *Excuse me* and *Sorry*.

1a/b [T 66] Students look at the photograph and then read and listen to the dialogue once or twice before repeating each line chorally and individually.

Have students practise the dialogue first in open then in closed pairs.

c Put some different times on the board. In closed pairs, students continue practising the dialogue, substituting times from the board. Go round and monitor.

2a/b [T 67] Students look at the photograph and then read and listen to the dialogue once or twice before repeating each line chorally and individually.

c Have students practise the dialogue first in open then in closed pairs.

Additional material

Workbook Unit 8
Exercise 10 Further practice of *I'm sorry* and *Excuse me*.

GRAMMAR SUMMARY

This is a whole-class activity. Read through the substitution tables with the students. You may like to have students close their books, and you write the tables on the board. You could leave gaps and elicit the answers for some of the substitution items.

Draw students' attention to the caution box. You may like to put it up on the board. It indicates to students that *do* and *go* take *-es*, not just *-s*, in the third person singular.

Then either do the **Exercise** as a class, or have students work in pairs and then check answers with the class.

Answers
1 When *does* he *go* to work?
2 He *goes* to work at nine o'clock.
3 *Does* he *go* to London?
4 Yes, he *does*.

Word List
Ask the students to turn to page 76 and go through the words with them. Ask them to learn the words for homework, and test them on a few in the following lesson.

Additional material

Workbook Unit 8
Exercise 9 Transport vocabulary.
Exercise 11 In this exercise students translate sentences containing the main grammar points presented in the unit.

UNIT 8 TAPESCRIPTS

Tapescript 60

Rita Libby is from Canada, but she lives in London. She isn't married. She works in a hospital. Rita has a car and usually drives to work. She leaves home at half past eight and arrives at the hospital at nine o'clock. She likes her job, but she likes the weekends, too. On Saturdays she sometimes goes shopping. She goes to the centre of London by train. On Sundays she eats in a restaurant with friends. She never cooks on Sundays.

Tapescript 61

Rita works in a hospital.
She arrives at the hospital at nine o'clock.
She likes her job.

Tapescript 62

1 He lives in Oxford.
2 She sometimes eats in a restaurant.
3 She goes to the centre of London by train.

Tapescript 63

A Does Rita live in London?
B Yes, she does.
A Does she like her job?
B Yes, she does.
A Does she go to work by train?
B No, she doesn't.
A Does she cook on Sundays?
B No, she doesn't.

Tapescript 64

1 Does he live in Manchester?
2 Does he work at home on Fridays?
3 Does he drive to London?
4 Does he play football?
5 Does he cook dinner for his friends?

Tapescript 65

Ivor Chomacki is from Poland, but now he lives and works in Oxford in England. He's a computer programmer and he likes his job very much. He's married. His wife's English and her name's Kate. They have two small daughters. In his free time he likes reading, and he sometimes plays tennis.

Tapescript 66

A Excuse me!
B Yes?
A Can you tell me the time, please?
B Certainly. It's ten past five.
A Thank you.

Tapescript 67

A Oh, I'm sorry!
B It's OK.
A Let me help you.
B Thanks. It's very kind of you.

UNIT 9

Daily routines – Present Simple negative (*he/she/it*) – Question words – Social English 2

Introduction to the Unit

This unit practises the negative forms of the third person Present Simple along with daily routines. The question words *What*, *When*, *Where*, and *Who* are revised and *Why* is introduced along with *because*. Language for greetings and farewells is introduced and practised in the Everyday English section.

Notes on the Unit

PRESENTATION

1a T68 Students look at the pictures, and read and listen to the two texts. Alternatively, you can play each text unseen first to see how much students understand, before they listen and read. However, don't ask comprehension questions as this is a presentation, not skills work as such.

You may want to explain new vocabulary after they have listened for the first time, in which case pause at the end of each text to explain the new words: *get up early*, *start work*, *every day*, *travel agency*, *to visit*.

b In pairs, students refer to the first text about Sam and complete the sentences with the appropriate verb. Go over the answers by asking individual students to read out a sentence each. Check pronunciation at the same time.

> ⚠️ Draw students' attention to the caution box. You may want to put it up on the board. It indicates that the third person singular Present Simple form of *have* is irregular.

Answers
2 He *teaches* in a secondary school.
3 He *has* two small children.
4 He *gets* up early.
5 He *has* breakfast at seven o'clock.
6 He *leaves* work at four o'clock.

c In pairs, students refer to the second text and complete the negative sentences about Andrea. Go over the answers, checking pronunciation. Make sure *doesn't* /dʌznt/ is pronounced correctly.

> ⚠️ Draw students' attention to the caution box. You may like to put it up on the board. It highlights the fact that the third person singular negative in the Present Simple is formed with *doesn't* plus the infinitive of the verb.

Answers
2 She *doesn't have* children.
3 She *doesn't get* up early.
4 She *doesn't have* breakfast.
5 She *doesn't leave* work at four o'clock.

2a T69 Students read and listen to the questions. *Why* will be new to them. Translate it into students' L1 if you can; if not, they should be able to understand it from context.

> ⚠️ Draw students' attention to the caution box. You may like to put it up on the board. It explains that *What does he do?* means the same as *What's his job?* If you like, you can tell students that the former is more common.

b T69 Students listen to the sentences again, and repeat them after you or the cassette, chorally and individually.

44

c Students match a question with an answer. *Because* is new here. Translate it if you can, and highlight the link with the question word *Why*.

d/e `T 70` Students listen and check their answers to the matching exercise. Then they practise the questions and answers in pairs.

> **Answers**
> 1 Where does Sam live?   c In London.
> 2 What does he do?   a He's a teacher.
> 3 When does he get up?   b At half past six.
> 4 Who does he teach?   e Children in a
>   secondary school.
> 5 Why does he like his job? d Because he likes
>   teaching children.

3a Students look back at the second text to complete the information about Andrea in note form.

> **Answers**
> Home: small flat in Rome
> Job: *works in a travel agency* or
>   *travel agent*
> Gets up: 8.45
> Starts work: *10.00*
> Lunch: a sandwich in a snack bar
> Leaves work: *7.00*
> Likes job because: interesting
> At weekends: visits her boyfriend, Roberto

b Students use the question words in **2a** to complete the questions.

> **Answers**
> 1 *Where* does Andrea live?
> 2 *What* does she do?
> 3 *When* does she start work?
> 4 *Who* does she visit at weekends?
> 5 *Why* does she like her job?

c In closed pairs, students ask and answer the questions using the notes in **3a**. Go round and monitor.

Go over the answers by having students ask and answer in open pairs across the class. Check grammar and pronunciation.

> **Answers**
> 1 Where does Andrea live? *In a small flat in Rome.*
> 2 What does she do? *She works in a travel agency.* or *She's a travel agent.*
> 3 When does she start work? *She starts work at ten o'clock.*
> 4 Who does she visit at weekends? *She visits her boyfriend, Roberto.*
> 5 Why does she like her job? *Because it's interesting.*

4 In this exercise students practise forming third person negative and affirmative sentences.

`T 71` Students listen to sentences about Sam and Andrea on the cassette. Pause the cassette after each sentence for students to either confirm the information or correct it, following the speech bubble examples in the Student's Book. You can call upon individual students to offer a correction first, then the whole class can repeat it.

> **Answers**
> Sam has three small children.
> *He doesn't have three small children. He has two small children.*
> Andrea works in a hospital.
> *She doesn't work in a hospital. She works in a travel agency.*
> Sam gets up at seven o'clock.
> *He doesn't get up at seven o'clock. He gets up at half past six.*
> Andrea doesn't have breakfast.
> *Yes, that's right.*
> Sam teaches on Tuesdays and Thursdays.
> *He doesn't teach on Tuesdays and Thursdays. He stays at home with his children.* or *He teaches on Mondays, Wednesdays, and Fridays.*
> Andrea has a salad for lunch.
> *She doesn't have a salad for lunch. She has a sandwich.*
> Andrea leaves work at six o'clock.
> *She doesn't leave work at six o'clock. She leaves work at seven o'clock.*

PRACTICE

1a This is another information gap activity. Divide students into A and B roles and have them look at the relevant pages.

If you think students can cope, they can do the

exercise orally in closed pairs. If not, put the As in pairs together and the Bs in pairs together to work out and write the questions they need to ask. Then As can form pairs with Bs and ask and answer their questions. Go round and monitor while they are doing this.

Go over the answers by calling on individual students to ask and answer in open pairs across the class.

Answers
A Where does Vannee live?
B She lives in Bangkok.
A Why does she like her job?
B Because she likes working with people.
A When does she start work?
B She starts work at 7.30.
A When does she have lunch?
B She has lunch at 12.30.
A When does she leave work?
B She leaves work at 3.30.

B Where's Vannee from?
A She's from Thailand.
B What's her job?/What does she do?
A She's a nurse.
B What time does she get up?
A She gets up at 6.00.
B When does she have breakfast?
A She has breakfast at 6.30.
B What does she have/eat for lunch?
A She has/eats fish and rice.
B What does she do at weekends?
A She visits her parents.

Additional material
Workbook Unit 9
Exercise 2 Further practice of question words.

2a Students read the text about Henry, then, in pairs or groups of three, work out how many hours Henry works. Check the answer, and see if any students can explain to you in English how they worked it out!

Answer
Henry works for nine hours every day (assuming a 15-minute break for tea).
8.00–11.00 = 3 hours
11.15–16.00 = 4 hours 45 minutes
16.15–17.30 = 1 hour 15 minutes

b Keep students in their pairs or threes to work on the true/false sentences either orally or in writing. Go round and monitor, then go over the answers with the class.

Answers
1 ✗ Henry doesn't get up late. He gets up early.
2 ✔
3 ✗ She doesn't work at the station.
4 ✗ She doesn't go to work by car. She goes to work by train.
5 ✔
6 ✗ Henry doesn't have lunch.
7 ✔

Additional material
Workbook Unit 9
Exercises 1, 3, and 4 Further practice of daily routines.

3a Students should write at least five questions to ask their partner. The questions may look a bit complicated, but all they need to do is to insert *do you* after the question word. (If you think they need more support, you could put them in pairs to devise the questions, then have them change partners to ask the questions.)

b In closed pairs, students ask and answer the questions.

c Go over the answers by calling on a few students to report what they found out about their partner to the class.

Additional idea
To check their questions and/or to change the focus, you could have the students ask you their questions in a class interview.

4 In pairs or groups, students correct the sentences. This is the first time that they have done this kind of exercise without having the correct sentence alongside the incorrect one or the mistake highlighted, so it may be a little harder. Check the answers and go over any problems with grammar.

Answers
1 He *doesn't* live in Hamburg.
2 Why *do you work* at home?
3 They *don't* learn English.
4 She *has* two cats.
5 What *do you* do?

5 Students match the questions and answers. Go over the answers by having students ask and answer in open pairs across the class.

LISTENING

1a **T 72** Play the cassette. Students listen to Henry talking about his brother.

b In pairs, students look at the true/false sentences and see how many they can do before you play the cassette again.

c **T 72** Play the cassette again for students to complete and check their answers. Go over the answers with the class.

Answers

1 ✔	3 ✘	5 ✔
2 ✘	4 ✘	

VOCABULARY

1a Students have to organize the vocabulary into six groups of three words. Explain this, using the example.

Put students into pairs to categorize the vocabulary. Then have students read out their groups of words. Write them on the blackboard.

Answers

baker	singer	journalist
what?	why?	who?
lunch	breakfast	dinner
train	car	bus
evening	morning	afternoon
go to bed	go shopping	go to work

b As revision, students test each other in closed pairs. One student closes their book and their partner gives them a word from one of the vocabulary groups in **1a**. The first student then has to try to remember the other two words in the group.

Additional material
Workbook Unit 9
Exercise 12 Vocabulary revision. Opposites.
Exercise 14 Crossword. Vocabulary revision.

EVERYDAY ENGLISH

Social English 2

This deals with simple greetings and farewells.

1a **T 73** Students look at the photo, and read and listen to the conversation once or twice.

b **T 73** Students repeat line by line after you or the cassette, chorally and individually. Make sure they use the appropriate intonation and sound friendly.

c Students practise the conversation in closed pairs.

Then draw students' attention to the tinted box which contains items for substitution. *Work* can be replaced by *life* or *the family*; *not bad* by *fine* or *very well*.

Students make more conversations using these variations.

2 **T 74** Follow the same procedure as for the conversation in **Exercise 1** above.

Weekend can be replaced by *evening* or *holiday*; *Monday* by *tomorrow* or *next week*.

Additional material
Workbook Unit 9
Exercise 11 Further practice of greetings and farewells.

GRAMMAR SUMMARY

This is a whole-class activity. Read through the substitution tables with the students. You may like to have students close their books, and you write the tables on the board. You could leave gaps and elicit the answers for some of the substitution items.

You could do the same with the prepositions, writing the sentences up on the board with gaps and eliciting the prepositions from the students.

> Draw students' attention to the caution box. You may like to put it up on the board. It reminds the students that *What do you do?* means the same as *What's your job?* (They were previously given the phrases in the third person.) You may wish to point out again that the second expression *What do you do?* is more common.

Then either do the **Exercise** as a class, or have students work in pairs and then check answers with the class.

Word List

Ask the students to turn to page 77 and go through the words with them. Ask them to learn the words for homework, and test them on a few in the following lesson.

Additional material

Workbook Unit 9

Exercises 5, 6, and 7 Further practice of the Present Simple, third person.

Exercise 10 Prepositions.

Exercise 13 In this exercise students translate sentences containing the main grammar points presented in the unit.

UNIT 9 TAPESCRIPTS

Tapescript 68

Sam Taylor lives in London. He is married and has two small children. He teaches in a secondary school. He gets up early and has breakfast at seven o'clock. He starts work at eight o'clock and leaves work at four o'clock. He likes his job because he likes teaching children. But he doesn't teach every day. On Tuesdays and Thursdays he stays at home with his children.

Andrea Taylor is Sam's sister. She doesn't have children. She's only twenty-three. And she doesn't live in Britain. She lives in Italy. She works in a travel agency in Rome. She doesn't get up early. She starts work at ten o'clock. She doesn't have breakfast. She has a sandwich for lunch at twelve o'clock. She leaves work at seven o'clock. She likes her job because it is very interesting. At weekends she visits her boyfriend, Roberto. He lives in Florence.

Tapescript 69

1 Where does Sam live?
2 What does he do?
3 When does he get up?
4 Who does he teach?
5 Why does he like his job?

Tapescript 70

1 Where does Sam live?
  In London.
2 What does he do?
  He's a teacher.
3 When does he get up?
  At half past six.
4 Who does he teach?
  Children in a secondary school.
5 Why does he like his job?
  Because he likes teaching children.

Tapescript 71

Sam lives in London.
Andrea lives in Britain.
Sam has three small children.
Andrea works in a hospital.
Sam gets up at seven o'clock.
Andrea doesn't have breakfast.
Sam teaches on Tuesdays and Thursdays.
Andrea has a salad for lunch.
Andrea leaves work at six o'clock.

Tapescript 72

Yeah, well our family lives in Hampstead. But my brother, his name's Terry, he lives in Wimbledon. That's in London, too. He doesn't live in Hampstead any more, because he has a job in Wimbledon now. Terry gets up early, at six o'clock, so he usually stays at home in the evenings. He likes reading and watching television. At weekends he relaxes. He goes shopping and visits his friends.

Tapescript 73

A Hi, Jon.
B Hello, Irene. Nice to see you.
A And you. How's work?
B Oh, not bad, thanks.

Tapescript 74

A Goodbye, Mike.
B Goodbye, Sally. Have a nice weekend!
A Thanks, Mike. Same to you.
B Thanks. See you on Monday.

UNIT 10

Houses, rooms, and furniture – Colours – *there is/are* – *any* – At the post office

Introduction to the Unit

This introduces colours and house vocabulary with *There is/are. Any* is also introduced for plural questions. A situational dialogue in the post office is introduced and practised in the Everyday English section.

Notes on the Unit

PRESENTATION

1a As a class, students talk briefly about where they live. You may need to explain *garden* and the difference between *house* and *flat*. Drawing them on the board is the easiest way.

b In closed pairs, students match the pictures and words. Check the answers with the class.

Answers					
kitchen	f	bathroom	c	balcony	b
bedroom	a	toilet	d		

c **T 75** Students listen to, and repeat, the words.

2a/b **T 76** Students either read and listen to the text, or they just listen and look at the picture of the living room on the previous page. Then they read the text and try to match the vocabulary to the picture. Check the answers and drill the pronunciation of the new vocabulary.

Answers					
sofa	1	chair	4	television	7
armchair	6	flowers	5	telephone	2
table	3	plant	8		

c **T 77** Have students read and listen to the sentences before you explain *There is* (singular) and *There are* (plural). If you can, translate *There is/are* into the students' language. If you can't do this, they should be able to pick up the meaning from the context.

d **T 77** Students repeat the sentences after you or the cassette.

e Students look at the picture of the living room again and talk about it, using *There is/are* and the new vocabulary. If possible, they should do this without looking at the text and words in **Exercise 2**.

This exercise could be done in closed pairs first, then all together as a class. Alternatively, if you think they need more help and support, keep it as a whole-class activity.

3a/b In this exercise, students practise the question form and short answers.

T 78 Students read and listen to the questions and answers, then listen again and repeat. Draw attention to the singular and plural forms and point out that we use *any* in questions in the plural.

c Students complete the questions and answers using those in **3a** as a model. Students can work alone or in pairs at first, or you can do this on the board as a whole-class activity.

d **T 79** Students listen and check their answers.

Answers	
Is there a sofa?	Yes, there *is.*
Is there a CD player?	No, there *isn't.*
Are there any armchairs?	Yes, there *are.*
Are there *any* photos?	No, there *aren't.*

e Students ask and answer the questions in **3a** and **3c** in open and/or closed pairs.

After a few minutes, ask students to cover the text. Have them ask and answer questions in closed pairs, just looking at the picture of the living room. They will probably have to think quite hard to do this. Go round and monitor.

4a Go over the pronunciation of the colours with the students.

b `T 80` Students read and listen to the questions and answers.

c `T 80` Students listen again and repeat.

d Students look at the picture of the living room again in pairs, and ask and answer about the colour of objects listed in the chart.

> **Answers**
> What colour is the sofa? It's blue.
> What colour is the table? It's brown.
> What colour is the telephone? It's white.
> What colour is the television? It's black.
> What colour are the chairs? They're brown.
> What colour are the armchairs? They're red.
> What colour are the plants? They're green.
> What colour are the flowers? They're yellow.

PRACTICE

1 In pairs, students choose the correct sentences. Check the answers with the class, and go over any grammar problems that arise.

> **Answers**
> | 1 | a | ✔ | 3 | a | ✘ | 5 | a | ✔ | 7 | a | ✔ |
> | | b | ✘ | | b | ✔ | | b | ✘ | | b | ✘ |
> | 2 | a | ✔ | 4 | a | ✔ | 6 | a | ✘ | 8 | a | ✘ |
> | | b | ✘ | | b | ✘ | | b | ✔ | | b | ✔ |

2 In pairs, students guess the colours using the prompts. They may not know all the words, but should get the colours anyway.

Go over the answers and check comprehension of vocabulary. (If you can't translate the new words, drawing quick pictures on the board is probably the easiest way to explain.)

> **Additional idea**
> Working in pairs or groups, students add one or two more words to each colour group.

This will help them to remember the names of the colours, and may also encourage them to ask you for the English names of other objects, thus increasing their vocabulary.

> **Additional material**
> **Workbook Unit 10**
> **Exercise 7** Revision of colours.

3 Students use *There is/are*, colours, and vocabulary to make sentences about the picture.

Draw attention to the examples and show them the position of the colour adjectives before the noun. You could contrast this with their own language if it differs in this respect.

> **Additional material**
> **Workbook Unit 10**
> **Exercises 1, 2, and 3** Further practice of house vocabulary with *There is/are*.

4 Students can do this exercise alone, writing the answers to the questions, or they can work in pairs, asking and answering the questions orally. Go over the possible answers by asking several individual students a question each.

5a Working in pairs or alone, students make questions by putting the words in the correct order.

b `T 81` Students listen and check their answers.

> **Answers**
> 1 What colour is your bedroom?
> 2 Are there any plants in your bathroom?
> 3 Is there a table in your living room?
> 4 What colour is your living room?
> 5 Are there any pictures in your kitchen?

> **Additional material**
> **Workbook Unit 10**
> **Exercises 4, 5, and 6** Further practice of questions with *Is there …?/Are there …?*

c In pairs, students ask and answer questions about each other's homes.

6 This is an information gap using picture differences. The pictures show two versions of a classroom. You may have covered words like *cassette player*, *board*, *desk*, etc. in 'Classroom language' in Unit 4. If not, you could pre-teach them or just feed in vocabulary as you monitor the activity.

Photocopy pictures A and B on page 67 of the Teacher's Book. Put the students into pairs and give an A and a B picture to each pair. Explain that they must not show their picture to their partner, but that they have to ask questions to find the eight differences.

Use the examples and the speech bubbles to explain and set up the activity. Either read through them with the class, or act them out with a student.

In closed pairs, students ask and answer about their pictures and note down the differences while you monitor. Feed in any vocabulary that students ask for (e.g. they may want to know *door*, *window*, *How many*, etc.).

Ask students to show each other their pictures to check their answers. Then go over the answers with the class, putting them up on the board.

Answers
In picture A, but not in B:
television, video, phone, 12 chairs (not 15), cassette player
In picture B, but not in A:
pictures, plants, 15 chairs (not 12), books

LISTENING

This listening reinforces the theme of classroom objects.

1a T82 Students listen to the cassette once and tick the items Yusef mentions.

b Students compare their answers in pairs.

c T82 Students listen again and check their answers. Play the cassette a third time if necessary.

Answers
two big tables ✔	twelve chairs ✔
a video	a television
a board ✔	pictures on the wall ✔
a cassette player ✔	a telephone
books ✔	two plants

d Students compare their classroom to Yusef's. You may need to go round the classroom, pointing out objects and asking individual students to volunteer a sentence.

READING

1a Allow students to read the text and see how much they understand before you explain the new vocabulary: *post office*, *secretary*, *miles*, *village*, *antique*, *painter*, and *happy*.

b Students say whether the sentences about Sarah and Colin are true or false. Have students correct the false sentences in pairs and then go over them with the class.

Answers
1 ✗ They live in an old house.
2 ✗ She drives five miles to work every day.
3 ✔
4 ✗ Sarah's mother is a painter. Sarah is a secretary.
5 ✗ The living room is yellow.
6 ✔

Additional material
Workbook Unit 10
Exercise 8 Further reading and writing practice.

EVERYDAY ENGLISH

At the post office

1a T83 Students look at the photo and read and listen to the conversations once or twice.

b T83 Students listen again and repeat the conversations line by line, chorally and individually.

Don't worry too much about money and prices. These are dealt with more fully in Unit 12.

c Students practise the conversations in closed pairs.

d Students make more conversations, using the items and prices in the boxes. Go round and monitor.

Additional material
Workbook Unit 10
Exercise 13 Revision of situational dialogues at the post office.

GRAMMAR SUMMARY

This is a whole-class activity. Read through the substitution tables with the students. You may like to have students close their books, and you write the tables on the board. You could leave gaps and elicit the answers for some of the substitution items.

Then either do the **Exercise** as a class, with students suggesting answers for the gaps, or have students work in pairs first and then check answers with the class.

Answers

Jenna   What colour *is* the living room?
Brenda *It's* blue, with a blue and white sofa.
Jenna   Nice. And what colour *are* the bedrooms?
Brenda They're yellow.
Jenna   *Are* there *any* pictures in the bedrooms?
Brenda Yes, there *are* two.
Jenna   *Is* there *a* television in your bedroom?
Brenda No, there *isn't!* The television's in the living room.

Word List

Ask the students to turn to page 77 and go through the words with them. Ask them to learn the words for homework, and test them on a few in the following lesson.

Additional material
Workbook Unit 10
Exercise 10 Prepositions.
Exercise 11 Word stress.
Exercise 12 In this exercise students translate sentences containing the main grammar points presented in the unit.

UNIT 10 TAPESCRIPTS

Tapescript 75

| living room | bedroom | toilet |
| kitchen | bathroom | balcony |

Tapescript 76

In my living room there's a sofa, and there are two armchairs. There's a table and four chairs. There are flowers on the table and there are two plants. There's a television and there's a telephone.

Tapescript 77

There's a sofa.   There are two armchairs.
There's a television.   There are two plants.

Tapescript 78

Is there a table?   Is there a video?
Yes, there is.   No, there isn't.

Are there any plants?   Are there any newspapers?
Yes, there are.   No, there aren't.

Tapescript 79

Is there a sofa?   Are there any armchairs?
Yes, there is.   Yes, there are.
Is there a CD player?   Are there any photos?
No, there isn't.   No, there aren't.

Tapescript 80

A What colour is the sofa?
B It's blue.
A What colour are the chairs?
B They're brown.

Tapescript 81

1 What colour is your bedroom?
2 Are there any plants in your bathroom?
3 Is there a table in your living room?
4 What colour is your living room?
5 Are there any pictures in your kitchen?

Tapescript 82

Well, there are eleven students in my English class, so in our classroom there are two big tables with twelve chairs. One chair is for our teacher, of course! On one wall there is a board for the teacher, and there are also some nice pictures on the wall. On the table there's a cassette player and there are also some books.

Tapescript 83

1 A Good morning.
   B Good morning.
   A Can I have five stamps for Italy, please?
   B Certainly. That's one pound twenty-five, please.
   A Thank you.
   B Thank you.

2 A Good morning.
   B Morning.
   A I'd like these postcards, please.
   B That's one pound, please.
   A Here you are … Thank you.
   B Thanks.

52

Prices – *How much is/are...?* – *Can I have ...?* – In a café

Introduction to the Unit

This unit practises mainly functional language. It revises numbers and introduces prices in pounds sterling with *How much is/are ...?* The extended Everyday English section practises requests and revises food vocabulary in a café situation.

Notes on the Unit

PRESENTATION

1a Students match the numbers and write them out for revision purposes.

Answers			
73	seventy-three	48	forty-eight
72	seventy-two	96	ninety-six
35	thirty-five	62	sixty-two
84	eighty-four	41	forty-one
27	twenty-seven		

b Students practise saying the numbers above. If they are rusty, put a few more on the board for them to say.

c **T 84** Students listen and tick the number they hear. Play the cassette twice or three times as necessary.

Go over the answers by having individual students say the numbers they heard. Write them on the board for the class to compare and check.

Answers	
seventeen	fifty
fifty-eight	seventy-nine
thirty	sixty-four
forty-two	

2a These conversations introduce *How much is/are ...?* and prices.

T 85 Students look at the picture and read and listen to the conversations once or twice.

b **T 85** Students listen again and repeat line by line. Then they practise the conversations in closed pairs.

c You may need to explain sterling currency and prices to the students. If so, put this on the board:

100 pence = £1
We write 50p.   We say 'fifty pence' or 'fifty p'.
We write £1.   We say 'one pound'.
We write £2.   We say 'two pounds'.
We write £1.50.   We say 'one pound fifty' (not 'fifty pence') or 'one fifty'.

In pairs, students write out the prices shown. Go over the answers by having individual students say the prices back to you. Write them on the board.

Answers	
55p	fifty-five p/pence
70p	seventy p/pence
£4.99	four pounds ninety-nine/four ninety-nine
£6.89	six pounds eighty-nine/six eighty-nine

3a In closed pairs, students look at the objects and say the prices. You may need to elicit the names of the objects first.

b **T 86** Students listen and check.

c In closed pairs, students ask and answer about the prices, as in the speech bubble example. Go over the answers by having students ask and answer in open pairs, while you and the rest of the class listen and check.

4

> **Additional idea**
>
> **T 87** You may like students to listen to these conversations with their books closed first. After each conversation, pause the cassette and ask what the person bought and how much it was.

a In pairs, students complete the three conversations with the phrases in the box.

b **T 87** Students listen and check their answers. Go over the answers by having students read out the conversations in open pairs across the class. Check pronunciation at the same time.

Answers
The phrases appear in the following order:
1 Good morning
  How much is that?
2 Can I help you?
  Can I have
  Here you are
3 How much are
  Anything else?
  That's two pounds sixty.

c Students read the conversations in closed pairs.

PRACTICE

1a Students do the arithmetic on their own.

b Demonstrate the first question or two with a student, referring the class to the speech bubble as a model. (This shows them that + is expressed as *and* which they will not know.) Then have them ask and answer in closed pairs, e.g. *How much is two pounds forty and ten p? Two pounds fifty.*

To check the answers, you ask the questions and the whole class replies.

Answers
47p + 31p = *78p*
£5.20 + £4.20 = *£9.40*
25p + 30p = *55p*
£6.50 + £7.20 = *£13.70*
65p + 40p = *£1.05*
£27 + £32.50 = *£59.50*

2 Students can do this exercise orally in pairs or in writing if they need more practice. Check the answers with the class.

Answers
1 How much is the champagne?
  It's sixteen pounds ninety-nine.
2 How much is the T-shirt?
  It's six pounds.
3 How much are the envelopes?
  They're one pound.
4 How much is the book?
  It's eight pounds ninety-nine.
5 How much are the stamps?
  They're 64p.
6 How much is the radio?
  It's forty-nine pounds fifty.

> **Additional material**
> **Workbook Unit 11**
> **Exercises 2 and 3** Further practice of prices.

3a/b **T 88** In pairs students complete the dialogue with the words in the box, then listen and check their answers. Go over the answers by having students read out the conversation in open pairs across the class. Check pronunciation at the same time.

Answers
Henry Good afternoon.
Polly Good afternoon. *Do* you have *Harper's and Queen*?
Henry No, we *don't*. But we *have Options* or *Elle*.
Polly How *much* is *Elle*?
Henry It's £2.10.
Polly OK.
Henry Anything *else*?
Polly Yes. *Can* I have a big blue notebook, please?
Henry *Here* you are. £2.10 and £1.50, *that's* £3.60, please.
Polly £3.60. Here you are. Thanks very *much*.
Henry Thank you. Goodbye.
Polly Bye!

> **Additional material**
> **Workbook Unit 11**
> **Exercise 4** Further shop dialogues.

4a/b This is an information gap activity for more practice in asking and answering about prices. Divide the students into As and Bs. As look at page 79, and Bs look at page 80. Students ask and answer in closed pairs, following the examples in the speech bubbles, to complete the missing prices.

b Have students check each other's answers in pairs before you go over the answers with the class.

> **Answers**
> Let students look at each other's pages.

c/d Divide the class into shop assistants and customers.

To get this activity off the ground, you could refer students to the conversations in **Exercise 4a** on page 57 and **Exercise 3a** on page 58 and tell them to use either or both of these as models. Alternatively, you may like to elicit the first two or three lines of a possible dialogue and write these on the board for the students to continue in their pairs.

Students change roles and roleplay more conversations. Go round and monitor.

> **Additional material**
> **Workbook Unit 11**
> **Exercise 1** Further practice of *How much …?* and prices.

VOCABULARY

1a/b Students match the opposites. Check the answers with the class by saying a word and having students give the opposite.

Students then test each other in pairs. One student closes their book. Their partner says a word from the list and they give the opposite. After five or six words, they change roles.

Check the answers with the class. Ask students to close their books. Say a word and have the class give you its opposite.

> **Answers**
>
> | | | | |
> |---|---|---|---|
> | early | late | get up | go to bed |
> | morning | evening | lovely | horrible |
> | white | black | go | stay |
> | old | new | he | she |

> **Additional material**
> **Workbook Unit 11**
> **Exercise 9** Vocabulary revision.

LISTENING

1a Ask students to look at the picture. Read the list of objects and prices with the students, quickly revising their pronunciation as this helps students with the listening task.

  T 89 Play the cassette. Students tick the prices they hear.

b Students compare answers in pairs.

c Play the cassette, twice more if necessary, before checking the answers with the class.

> **Answers**
>
> | | |
> |---|---|
> | Spanish newspaper | £1.15 |
> | birthday card | £1.10 |
> | three postcards | 90p |
> | three stamps | 75p |
> | total | £3.90 |

EVERYDAY ENGLISH

In a café

1a In pairs or groups of three, students match the words and pictures as best they can. Go over the answers and practise the pronunciation of the words at the same time.

> **Answers**
>
> | | | | |
> |---|---|---|---|
> | 1 | orange juice | 2 | cheese |
> | 3 | piece of apple pie | 4 | ice-cream |
> | 5 | cup | 6 | ham |
> | 7 | egg | 8 | cake |

b **T 90** Students look at the photo. You can pre-teach *waiter* and *waitress*. Students then read and listen to the conversations.

> **Additional idea**
> **T 90** Instead of having students read and listen, you could ask them to cover the text and to listen for what food and drinks people order, and their prices. Play the cassette, pausing after each dialogue for students to tell you what they heard.
>
> Then students can read the conversations in full (and listen again if they want to) before practising in pairs.

c **T 90** Students listen and repeat after you or the cassette.

d Students practise the conversations in closed pairs while you monitor.

Additional idea

Before they start the roleplay in **Exercise 1e**, you may like to practise polite intonation, using the example sentences in the box. Model and drill the sentences chorally and individually. Make sure students start off high. It can help to exaggerate the intonation at first, especially if the students' mother tongue does not employ a very wide voice range.

For example,

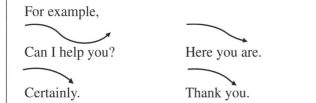

Can I help you?   Here you are.

Certainly.   Thank you.

---

e Students roleplay conversations in a café, referring to the menu and using the phrases in the boxes if necessary. You could put the students into groups of three for a change, and have a waiter/waitress and two customers. If possible, you could organize the room in such a way that the groups could stand up and act out the roleplay, while you monitor or take part. Afterwards one or two groups could perform in front of the class if they want to.

Additional material

Workbook Unit 11

Exercises 5, 6, and 7 Further practice of café dialogues.

GRAMMAR SUMMARY

This is a whole-class activity. Read through the substitution tables with the students. You may like to have students close their books, and you write the tables on the board. You could leave gaps and elicit the answers for some of the substitution items.

Then either do the **Exercise** as a class, with students suggesting answers, or have students work in pairs and check answers with the class.

Answers
1 c,   2 e,   3 d,   4 f,   5 a,   6 b

Word List

Ask the students to turn to page 77 and go through the words with them. Ask them to learn the words for homework, and test them on a few in the following lesson.

Additional material

Workbook Unit 11

Exercise 8 Making negatives with *but*.

Exercise 10 In this exercise students translate sentences containing the main grammar points presented in the unit.

Exercise 11 Articles.

UNIT 11 TAPESCRIPTS

Tapescript 84

seventeen   thirty   fifty   sixty-four
fifty-eight   forty-two   seventy-nine

Tapescript 85

1 A How much is the red pen?
  B It's ninety-nine pence.
  A How much are the brown envelopes?
  B They're one pound fifty.

2 A Can I have a *Daily Express*, please?
  B Here you are.
  A How much is that?
  B That's thirty p, please.

Tapescript 86

thirty p   ninety-nine p
one pound thirty   one pound fifty
seventy-five p   forty p

Tapescript 87

1 Henry   Good morning, Mary.
  Mary   Good morning, Henry. Can I have two red pens, please?
  Henry   Here you are.
  Mary   How much is that?
  Henry   One pound ninety-eight.
  Mary   Here you are … Thanks. See you tomorrow.
  Henry   See you. Bye.

2 Rita   Good afternoon.
  Henry   Good afternoon. Can I help you?
  Rita   Yes. Can I have *Woman and Home*, please?
  Henry   Here you are. That's one pound thirty. Anything else?
  Rita   No, thanks.

3 Michael Good morning.
  Henry   Good morning.
  Michael How much are the small notebooks?
  Henry   They're seventy-five p.
  Michael OK. Two, please.
  Henry   Anything else?
  Michael Yes. A magazine. Do you have *Journalism Today*?
  Henry   Yes. Here you are. One pound fifty and one pound ten. That's two pounds sixty.

Tapescript 88

Henry   Good afternoon.
Polly   Good afternoon. Do you have *Harper's and Queen*?
Henry   No, we don't. But we have *Options* or *Elle*.
Polly   How much is *Elle*?
Henry   It's £2.10.
Polly   OK.
Henry   Anything else ?
Polly   Yes. Can I have a big blue notebook, please?
Henry   Here you are. £2.10 and £1.50, that's £3.60, please.
Polly   £3.60. Here you are. Thanks very much.
Henry   Thank you. Goodbye.
Polly   Bye!

Tapescript 89

Tourist Good morning. Do you have any Spanish newspapers?
Henry   Yes, we have *El Mundo* or *El País*.
Tourist How much is *El Mundo*?
Henry   It's one pound fifteen.
Tourist OK. And can I have that birthday card, the card with the picture of the boy and the birthday cake?
Henry   Here you are. It's one pound ten. Anything else?
Tourist Yes, how much are these postcards?
Henry   They're 30 pence each.
Tourist Can I have three, please?
Henry   Certainly. Do you want stamps, too?
Tourist Oh, yes. Three stamps for Spain, please.
Henry   That's 75 pence then. Is that everything?
Tourist Yes, thanks. How much is that?
Henry   Let me see. That's £3.90.

Tapescript 90

1 A Good morning. Can I help you?
  B Yes. Can I have a cheese sandwich and a cup of tea, please?
  A Certainly. Here you are. Anything else?
  B No, thanks.
  A That's two pounds, please.
  B Thanks.
  A Thank you.

2 A Hello.
  B Hi. Can I have a pizza and a salad, please?
  A Anything to drink?
  B Yes. An orange juice and a mineral water, please.
  A OK.
  B How much is that?
  A Five pounds eighty-five, please.
  B Here you are … Thanks.
  A Thank you.

UNIT 12

Seasons – Months – Adverbs of frequency – Prepositions – At the bank

Introduction to the Unit

This unit introduces the seasons and months along with adverbs of frequency. It also offers further practice of the Present Simple. Situational dialogues at the bank are introduced and practised in the Everyday English section.

Notes on the Unit

PRESENTATION

1a In pairs, students read the texts and try to match them to the pictures. They won't know all the vocabulary, but should understand enough to do the task.

b **T 91** Students read and listen to the texts in the correct order and check their answers. Go over the answers by asking questions, e.g. *Which photo is spring?* to elicit the answers, e.g. *Number one*.

New vocabulary in the texts:
Adverbs of frequency: *always* and *often*.
Text 1: *spring, to grow*.
Text 2: *summer, to love, hot, long, warm, beach*.
Text 3: *autumn, favourite, season, to walk, woods*.
Text 4: *winter, cold, wet, grey, short*.

Answers			
Picture 1	spring	Picture 3	autumn
Picture 2	summer	Picture 4	winter

2a Students fill in the months as best they can.

b **T 92** Students listen and check their answers. Then they listen again and repeat.

Answers			
Spring	**Summer**	**Autumn**	**Winter**
March	June	September	December
April	July	October	January
May	August	November	February

c Let students practise saying the months quietly to themselves first. Then, with books closed if possible, have students say the months round the class, with individual students saying a month each in turn. (You could repeat the procedure, this time pointing to students at random, who then have to say the next month in the sequence.)

d If you can, translate *Christmas*, *New Year*, and *Easter* into students' L1, then quickly practise the pronunciation, so that students can ask all five questions in closed pairs.

(With some non-European students, you may have to do the first three questions with the class if they are unfamiliar with these festivals. They could talk about their own festivals and when they occur instead.)

Additional idea

You can extend questions 4 and 5 in **3d** above by doing them as a class 'mingle' activity. Students can stand up and ask everyone in the class the two questions to find out which month the most students have birthdays in and which month the most students take their summer holidays in.

When students have finished, you can put the twelve months on the board and have each student give you some information about one, e.g. *Serena's birthday is in March.*, *Kevin's summer holiday is in August.*, *Toros goes on holiday in August.* Write *B* for birthday, and *H* for holiday beside the relevant months to summarize the information.

---

e Students talk about their favourite season. You could have students ask and answer in closed pairs and then ask individual students to tell the class which is their favourite season and why. Alternatively, you could tell the class which is your favourite season and why, before asking a few students to tell the class about their preferences.

3 Students know three of the adverbs of frequency already (*usually*, *sometimes*, and *never*) as these came up in Unit 8. *Usually* is slightly different in that it expresses habit rather than frequency, but treat it as the same for now. One common negative expression, *don't often*, is introduced here.

a Go through the sentences with the students. You can write up the following percentages with the adverbs to help with comprehension:

always	100%	sometimes	40%
usually	90%	don't often	20%
often	70%	never	0%

Students fill in the gaps with adverbs to make true sentences about themselves. This exercise also demonstrates the position of the adverbs *before* the verb.

⚠️ Draw students' attention to the caution box. You may want to put it up on the board. It points out the fact that adverbs of frequency come before the verb, not after it. (Some adverbs can also go at the end of the sentence, but it is not necessary to mention this now.)

b Students exchange books and read someone else's sentences. Ask a few students to read out one or two sentences, then ask if anyone else in the class has the same sentence(s).

PRACTICE

1 In pairs students complete the puzzle and discover the month that reads vertically down.

Answers
```
        J U L Y
    M A R C H
        N O V E M B E R
    A U G U S T
    M A Y
D E C E M B E R
F E B R U A R Y
```

2a Students make sentences about themselves.

b/c Put students into groups to compare their habits. Students read their sentences aloud and the others compare theirs and try to find similarities. They then report any similarities back to the class, following the speech bubble examples.

3a Students ask and answer in pairs and complete the questionnaire.

b This exercise practises the third person singular forms. Students change partners and ask and answer about their previous partners.

c/d Ask one or two individual students to tell the class about their first partners. Then, if further practice is needed, have students write sentences either in class or at home.

4 This is an information gap activity. Divide students into As and Bs. As stay on page 65 and Bs turn to page 78. Students ask and answer questions about Gareth and Marie, and fill in the missing frequency adverbs. Ask students if any of Gareth and Marie's habits are the same. (Answer: They both sometimes watch television in the evenings.)

Go over the answers by calling on individual students to make one complete sentence about Gareth or Marie, using the prompts in the chart.

Answers
Gareth
He usually works late.
He sometimes watches television.
He never cooks dinner.
He doesn't often drink coffee in the evenings.
He doesn't often go out in the evenings.
Marie
She doesn't usually work late.
She sometimes watches television.
She always cooks dinner.
She never drinks coffee in the evenings.
She usually goes out in the evenings.

Additional material

Workbook Unit 12

Exercises 3 and 4 Further practice of the Present Simple third person with adverbs of frequency.

5 This practises prepositions with days of the week, seasons, and months. Students fill in the gaps in class or for homework.

Answers
Susie Cooper loves sport. *On* Wednesdays she watches football on television. Susie goes dancing *on* Fridays. She usually goes swimming *at* weekends. *In* summer she plays tennis and *in* winter she goes skiing. She plays golf *in* spring and autumn. But *in* August she goes *on* holiday. She relaxes *in* Spain and doesn't do any sports!

PRONUNCIATION

This revises the pronunciation of the months.

1a/b **T 93** Students complete the chart, then listen and check their answers. Go over the answers with the class.

Answers

●	●●	●●	●●●	●●●●
March	April	*July*	September	January
May	*August*		October	*February*
June			November	
			December	

c Students practise saying the months quietly to themselves. Then call on individual students each to say a month in sequence around the class.

LISTENING

1a **T 94** Students listen to John and tick the correct answers in the chart. Play the cassette two or three times, as necessary.

b Allow students to check their answers in pairs after each listening. Go over the answers with the class.

Answers

	always	usually	often	sometimes	never
go to work by train?	☐	☐	☐	✔	☐
get up early?	✔	☐	☐	☐	☐
have tea for breakfast?	☐	✔	☐	☐	☐
visit friends at weekends?	☐	☐	☐	☐	✔
go shopping on Saturdays?	☐	☐	✔	☐	☐

2a In pairs, students read the song and the sentences, then put the sentences in the correct places. If students are having problems, draw their attention to the rhymes.

b **T 95** Students listen to the song and check their answers. They can sing along if they want to.

Answers
The sentences appear in this order:
2   When winter days are long and grey, ...
4   Like the flowers in the spring, ...
3   Summer days are long and warm, ...
1   We walk together under autumn trees.

READING

In pairs students read the text and put the sentences in the correct places. Go over the answers with the class. The following words will be new to the students: *baker's shop*, *tourist*, *bread*, *to clean*, *to look after*, *open* (adj).

Answers
The sentences go into the text in the following order:
2   In summer the Volpes work twelve hours a day, and at weekends, too.
4   So the Volpes only work seven hours a day and on Sundays they get up late and stay at home.
1   The baker's shop is not open in winter.
3   Well, Signor and Signora Volpe go to Rome!

Additional idea

If you like, you could ask the following comprehension questions:
Where do Signor and Signora Volpe live? (In Tonda, Italy.)
What do they do? / What are their jobs? (They're bakers. / They have a baker's shop.)
What do they do in summer? (They work twelve hours a day, and at weekends, too.)
What do they do in spring and autumn? (They only work seven hours a day and on Sundays they get up late and stay at home.)
What do they do in winter? (Signor Volpe cleans the shop. Signora Volpe works in the house and looks after the children. They go on holiday.)
Where do they go on holiday? (They go to Rome.)

Additional material

Workbook Unit 12
Exercise 9 and 10 Further reading and writing practice on the seasons.

EVERYDAY ENGLISH

At the bank

1a **T 96** Students look at the picture and read and listen to the conversations. At first they should simply listen and not write. The following vocabulary will be new: *traveller's cheque, passport, to change some money, dollar, to sign.*

b Students work in pairs to complete the conversations as best they can.

c **T 96** Let them listen again once or twice and check the answers with each other, then go over the answers with the class.

Students listen and repeat key sentences with new vocabulary after you or the cassette.

Answers
1 A Good afternoon. Can I *help* you?
  B *Can* I change these traveller's cheques, please?
  A Certainly. Can I see your passport, please?
  B *Here* you *are*.
  A Thank you. Sign here, please. Right, that's twenty, *forty*, sixty, *eighty* pounds.
  B Thank you. *Goodbye*.

2 A Good morning. Can I *change* some money, please?
  B How much do you want to change?
  A A *hundred* and fifty dollars, please.
  B OK ... Sign *here*, please.
    Thank you. That's twenty, forty, sixty, eighty, a hundred *pounds*.
  A Thank you. Goodbye.

d In closed pairs, students practise the conversations. Then they can roleplay more conversations, using different currencies. If you can, give them the approximate current exchange rates of their own currencies against sterling. Alternatively, you can put some currencies and approximate exchange rates on the board and your students may be able to suggest some more. For example:

Approximate exchange rates
£1 = 1 dollar 50 cents (US)
    10 French francs
    2 German marks
    150 Japanese yen
    200 Spanish pesetas.

You might like to teach them *What's the exchange rate? It's (10 francs) to the pound.*

Additional material

Workbook Unit 12
Exercise 14 Further practice of bank dialogues.

GRAMMAR SUMMARY

This is a whole-class activity. Read through the substitution tables with the students. You may like to have students close their books, and you write the tables on the board. You could leave gaps and elicit the answers for some of the substitution items.

Then either do the **Exercise** as a class, with students suggesting answers, or have students work in pairs and then check answers with the class.

Answers
1 He always visits his mother on Sundays.
2 You never cook dinner.
3 They don't often go to bed early.
4 We usually go skiing in winter.
5 She sometimes drives to the English class.

Word List

Ask the students to turn to page 77 and go through the words with them. Ask them to learn the words for homework, and test them on a few in the following lesson.

Additional material

Workbook Unit 12

Exercise 8 Pronunciation: vowels and diphthongs.

Exercises 11 and 12 Weather vocabulary.

Exercise 13 Vocabulary revision.

Exercise 15 In this exercise students translate sentences containing the main grammar points presented in the unit.

UNIT 12 TAPESCRIPTS

Tapescript 91

1 We like spring. We have a big garden, and the plants and flowers start to grow in March. In spring, we usually work and relax in the garden at weekends. We never go on holiday in spring!

2 I love summer. It's always hot in Granada. I go swimming every day, and I like going out with my friends in the long, warm evenings. I don't often stay at home in summer! I sometimes go to the beach with my family for two weeks in August.

3 Our favourite season is autumn. We like walking and we often walk in the woods near our house. We like the colours of the trees in October – brown, yellow, orange, and gold.

4 Winter in Belgium is often cold, wet, and grey. The days are short. But it's my favourite season because I go skiing in January. I usually go skiing in the Alps. I love the sun and snow.

Tapescript 92

January	April	July	October
February	May	August	November
March	June	September	December

Tapescript 93

March	April	July	September	January
May	August		October	February
June			November	
			December	

Tapescript 94

Interviewer	Good morning, John.
John	Good morning. So you have some questions for me.
Interviewer	Yes, that's right. Er, do you go to work by train?
John	Sometimes. I drive to work when I have the car, but when my wife has the car I go by train.
Interviewer	Do you get up early for work, then?
John	Oh, always. I get up at six o'clock and at weekends, too.
Interviewer	Oh really? And tell me, what do you have for breakfast? Do you have tea for breakfast?
John	I usually have tea for breakfast, but coffee's all right, too.
Interviewer	Right. Now, let's talk about the weekend. Do you visit friends at weekends?
John	Never! In my job I talk to people all week. I relax with my family at weekends.
Interviewer	What about shopping? Do you go shopping on Saturdays?
John	Yes, we often go shopping on Saturdays. I don't like shopping, but my wife and daughter love it.
Interviewer	OK. Thank you, John.

Tapescript 95

Song for all Seasons

You and me, always together,
Me and you, together forever,
You and me, always together, me and you.

When winter days are long and grey,
We dance in the snow.
Like flowers in the spring,
We watch our love grow.

You and me, always together,
Me and you, together forever,
You and me, always together, me and you.

Summer days are long and warm
With roses red and golden sun.
When the summer season leaves,
We walk together under autumn trees.

You and me, always together,
Me and you, together forever,
You and me, always together, me and you.

Tapescript 96

1 A Good afternoon. Can I help you?
   B Can I change these traveller's cheques, please?
   A Certainly. Can I see your passport, please?
   B Here you are.
   A Thank you. Sign here, please. Right, that's twenty, forty, sixty, eighty pounds.
   B Thank you. Goodbye.

2 A Good morning. Can I change some money, please?
   B How much do you want to change?
   A A hundred and fifty dollars.
   B OK … Sign here, please … Thank you. That's twenty, forty, sixty, eighty, a hundred pounds.
   A Thank you. Goodbye.

STOP AND CHECK 2 UNITS 6-12

This Stop and Check section allows students to revise what they have learnt so far. It can be used in a number of ways.

- You can set it in class as an informal progress test, and take in their work to correct.
- You can put students in groups to work on the exercises. They can then score their own or another student's answers as you go over the answers with the class.
- You can give the written parts for homework. Students can go over their answers in small groups in the next lesson, before doing the listening and speaking exercises with you in class.

It can be very productive for students to work in groups and try to persuade their peers of the right answer. Many previous lessons are recalled. It also takes the stress out of a 'test' situation, and with all the group discussion everyone should have a reasonably high score!

When you go over the answers with the class, you can take the opportunity to remind students of the language items covered.

STOP AND CHECK 2

Tapescript 97

My name's Derek Warrick. I'm forty-seven. My mother's name is Pat and she is sixty-eight. My father's name is Ken. He's seventy-two.
I'm a husband and father. My wife's name is Linda and she is, er thirty-nine, I think. We have three children, two sons, and a daughter. There's James. He's fourteen. His brother's name is Thomas. He's eleven. Our daughter's name is Emma, and she's eight.

Tapescript 98

mother
the sofa
Can I have a sandwich?
cup of tea
I'm from London.
He's at work.
cheese and ham salad
She drives to work
eight o'clock
There are four armchairs in my living room.

Tapescript 99

father
the computer
Can I have a salad?
cup of coffee
I'm from Stuttgart.
She's at work.
apple and orange pie
She drives to school.
nine o'clock
There are two plants in my living room.

PHOTOCOPIABLE MATERIAL

Identities for Practice Exercise 2b, Unit 2, on page 12 of the Student's Book.

NAME	Yoshi (m)
	Kumiko (f)
COUNTRY	Japan

NAME	Patrick (m)
	Gail (f)
COUNTRY	Ireland

NAME	Fernando (m)
	Elisabet (f)
COUNTRY	Spain

NAME	Pierre (m)
	Alice (f)
COUNTRY	France

NAME	Mike (m)
	Carol (f)
COUNTRY	England

NAME	Marco (m)
	Donatella (f)
COUNTRY	Italy

NAME	Robert (m)
	Nancy (f)
COUNTRY	the United States

NAME	Erol (m)
	Fatma (f)
COUNTRY	Turkey

NAME	Gareth (m)
	Morgan (f)
COUNTRY	Wales

NAME	Suzanna (m)
	István (f)
COUNTRY	Hungary

NAME	Calum (m)
	Fiona (f)
COUNTRY	Scotland

NAME	Luis (m)
	Fátima (f)
COUNTRY	Brazil

Pictures for Student A and Student B for Presentation Exercise 3, Unit 6, on page 26 of the Student's Book.

Student A

Student B

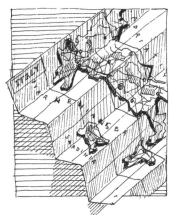   

  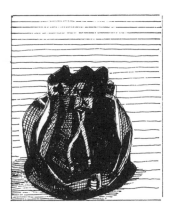 

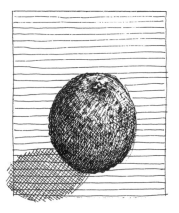 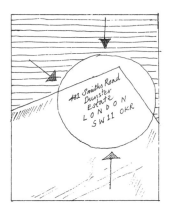 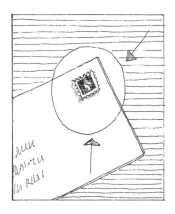 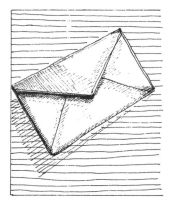

Identities for Student A and Student B, Stop and Check 1, Exercise 7b, on page 31 of the Student's Book.

Student A

NAME:	(f) Alison Fraser (m) James Fraser
COUNTRY:	Scotland
JOB:	actor/actress
WIFE'S/HUSBAND'S NAME:	(f) Alison (m) James
WIFE'S/HUSBAND'S JOB:	television producer
CHILDREN:	two daughters

Student B

NAME:	(f) Jenna Cline (m) Jason Cline
COUNTRY:	the United States
JOB:	supermarket manager
WIFE'S/HUSBAND'S NAME:	(f) Jenna (m) Jason
WIFE'S/HUSBAND'S JOB:	dentist
CHILDREN:	a son

Pictures for Student A and Student B for Practice Exercise 6, Unit 10, on page 53 of the Student's Book.

Picture A

Picture B

WORKBOOK KEY

This Workbook key may be photocopied for classroom use. It may not be adapted, printed, or sold without the written permission of Oxford University Press.

UNIT 1

1 Hello, Ann./Hi, John. How are you?/Fine, thanks. And you?/Very well, thanks.

2 a   How are you?   b   My name's John.
   c   What's your name?   d   This is Tom.

3 b   This is a   c   is a telephone
   d   This is a television. e   This is a football.
   f   This is a video.   g   This is a radio.
   h   This is a hamburger.

4 a   name   b   How/Fine/you/Fine, thanks.   c   this is/Hello

5 a   Hello. My name's David Black. What's your name?/Alec. Alec Williams.
   b   Hello, Linda. How are you?/Fine, thanks. And you?/Fine, thanks.
   c   Sushi, this is Ben. Ben, this is Sushi./Hello, Ben./Hello, Sushi.

6 a   nine   b   eighteen   c   fourteen   d   twelve
   e   seven   f   twenty   g   sixteen   h   five
   i   eleven   j   eight

7 a   seven   b   nine   c   eight   d   twelve
   e   ten   f   eighteen   g   twenty   h   seventeen
   i   six   j   sixteen

8
```
     T H I R T E E N
   T W E N T Y
     E I G H T
     L
 F I V E
 S E V E N
```

9
```
M  T E N N I S  N  P  A  Q
A  H Z L A M N Z W R  Y
F  I H A M B U R G E  R
G  S E I E H H F D Q  A
   T E L E P H O N E  D
S  A L U V T W H G J  I
D  F O O T B A L L  C  O
```

UNIT 2

1 b   Italy   c   Japan   d   Spain   e   England   f   France

2 a   Brazil   b   Hungary   c   Britain   d   Turkey

3 Clockwise from top of page: Scotland, England, Wales

4 a   France   b   Hungary   c   Japan   d   Spain
   e   Italy   f   England   g   Scotland   h   Germany

5 b   her/Antonella/she/Italy
   c   her/Fernanda/she/Brazil
   d   What's his/His name's Bill./Where's he/He's/England
   e   What's his name? His name's Rick. Where's he from? He's from the United States.
   f   What's her name? Her name's Kirsty. Where's she from? She's from Scotland.

6 b – 5, c – 1, d – 2, e – 4

7 a   What's your/are/from/I'm from
   b   Hello(Hi)/How/Fine/you/thanks/this/She's from/Hello(Hi)/Hello/(Hi)

8 a   teacher   b   Chârtres   c   Edinburgh, in Scotland
   d   taxi driver   e   Liverpool   f   the centre of London

9 a   My name's Tom.   b   I'm from Italy.
   c   You're a teacher.   d   What's your name?
   e   She's from Spain.   f   He's a doctor.
   g   Where's Luc from?   h   I'm from Wales.

UNIT 3

1 c   What's his job? He's a policeman.
   d   What's his job? He's a hairdresser.
   e   What's his job? He's a travel agent.
   f   What's her job? She's a student.
   g   What's her job? She's a teacher.
   h   What's his job? He's a shop assistant.

2
```
   S H O P   A S S I S T A N T
     D O C T O R
 T R A V E L   A G E N T
   T A X I   D R I V E R
   T E A C H E R
 H O U S E W I F E
         M
     H A I R D R E S S E R
 S T U D E N T
```

3 a   Where's she from?   b   What's her address?
   c   What's her phone number?   d   How old is she?
   e   What's her job?   f   Is she married?

4 a   No, she isn't.   b   Yes, she is.   c   No, she isn't.
   d   Yes, she is.   e   No, she isn't.   f   Yes, she is.
   g   Yes, she is.

6 a   Is he 28?   b   Are you a doctor?   c   Is he married?
   d   Am I from Japan?   e   Is she a travel agent?
   f   Are you married?   g   Is he 18?   h   Is she from Italy?

7 b – 3, c – 2, d – 1, e – 6, f – 5

8 a   am/am not   b   is   c   am/am not   d   is not
   e   is   f   is not   g   am/am not   h   is/is not

9 a   Ken isn't married.   b   Where's she from?
   c   I'm from Hungary.   d   I'm not a policeman.
   e   You're from Brazil.

10
a You are not a housewife.
b New York is not in Italy.
c The hospital is in the centre of the city.
d I am 28.
e You are a travel agent.

11 b forty-seven   c sixty   d seventy-four
e thirty-eight   f fifty-five   g one hundred
h eighty   i ninety-two   j sixty-three

12 b seventy-five   c fifty   d ninety-nine
e sixty-two   f sixty-six   g eighty-three
h twenty-seven   i forty-four   j forty-eight

UNIT 4

1 a son   b father   c brother   d daughter
e parents   f mother   g husband   h sister
i children

2 a ✔   b ✘ Andrew and Susan are Fiona's children.
c ✘ Andrew is Susan's brother.
d ✔   e ✘ Robin and Fiona are Andrew's parents.

3 c They're policemen.   d They're hairdressers.
e She's a taxi driver.   f They're shop assistants.
g He's a teacher.   h She's a housewife.

4 Top row: Winston
Second row: Neville/Daphne/Jessica/Robert
Third row: Darren

5 a Darren   b Neville   c Elizabeth
d Neville, Daphne, and Jessica   e Robert

6 a Suzanna Nagy   b Fritz Langer   c Suzanna Nagy
d Paulo Andrade   e Suzanna Nagy   f Fritz Langer
g Paulo Andrade   h Fritz Langer

7 a is   b P   c P   d is   e is   f P
g P   h P

8 a This is Pam's tennis racket.   b This is Simon's pen.
c This is Tessa's notebook.   d This is Kumiko's football.
e This is David's dictionary.

9 a s   b 's   c s   d 's   e 's   f ✘

10 a teacher   b twenty-two   c what
d dictionary   e student

11 a hundred – 100, fifty-nine – 59, twenty-eight – 28, fourteen – 14,
sixty-seven – 67, ninety-nine – 99, seventy-six – 76, forty – 40,
thirty-one – 31

12 a is   b are   c are   d is   e are   f are
g is   h are

13 Under *pen*: France, wife
Under *teacher*: student, daughter, children
Under *address*: cassette, Japan

14 What's this in English? It's a dictionary./Sorry. Can you say it
again, please?/Certainly. Dictionary./Can you spell it, please?
D-I-C-T-I-O-N-A-R-Y.

UNIT 5

1 2 cake   3 tea   4 water   5 bananas
6 wine   7 pizza   8 oranges   9 coffee
10 chocolate   11 salad   12 sandwiches   13 meat (chicken)
14 apples   15 beer

6 a do   b is/is   c Is/is   d are   e Do/do   f Are

7 a Yes, they do.   b Yes, they do.   c No, they don't.
d Yes, they do.   e No, they don't.   f Yes, they do.
g No, they don't.   h Yes, they do.

8 a Do you like pizza?   b Do they work in a hospital?
c Do you drink coffee?   d Do they live in Madrid?
e Do you eat meat?

9 a Do they drink wine?
b Do they eat apples?
c Do they like classical music?
d Do they live in the centre of Rome?
e Do they drink beer at weekends?
f Do they work in a bank?

10 b are   c is   d is   e are   f is
g Are   h are

11 Can I have a coffee, please? Certainly, here you are.
Are they married? Yes, they are.
Do they like pop music? Yes, they do.
Who's this? It's my sister.
Are you from Germany? Yes, I am.
What's his job? He's a doctor.
Where are you from? I'm from Italy.

12 your/meet/are/from/live/from/I'm/job/a/work/Do

UNIT 6

1 a an   b a   c an   d an   e a   f a
g a   h an   i a   j an

3 a Do you have a brother?   b Do they have a radio?
c Do you have a sister?   d Do they have a dictionary?
e Do you have a pen?   f Do you have a television?

4 a her   b Her   c Their   d His   e Her   f their

5 a My   b your   c your   d my   e your

6 b Joe's car is old.
c Ken's umbrella is big.
d Linda's computer is expensive.
e Luc's television is cheap.
f Alberto's radio is small.

7 good – food, beautiful – old buildings, friendly – people, small –
streets, new – shops, interesting – city

9 1b, 2b, 3a, 4b, 5a, 6b

10 b Friday [5]   c Tuesday [2]   d Thursday [4]
e Sunday [7]   f Wednesday [3]   g Saturday [6]

12
```
P  O  S  T  C  A  R  D
H           O
O     F  I  F  T  Y
N     F           E
E     E           X
   H  A  V  E     P
N  O              E
S  P  E  L  L     N
P     I           S
I     T  A  X  I
T     M           V
M  A  G  A  Z  I  N  E
L     P     N
```

STOP AND CHECK 1

1 b Where's he from?   c How old is he?
  d What's his address?   e What's his phone number?
  f Is he married?   g What's his job?/What does he do?

3 b Yes, they are.   c No, they don't.
  d Yes, they do.   e No, it isn't.

4 b No, I'm not.   c No, I don't.
  d Yes, I do.   e Yes, it is.

5 your/are/I'm/have/On/Do/Yes

6 Days: Wednesday, Tuesday, Friday, Saturday
  Food: sandwich, apple, chocolate, salad, meat
  Drink: tea, beer, wine, coffee, milk
  Family: mother, father, sister, wife, daughter
  Places: hospital, hotel, school, bank, factory
  Adjectives: big, interesting, friendly, small, cheap

UNIT 7

1 b singing   c dancing   d eating in restaurants
  e listening to music   f reading   g swimming
  h cooking   i watching television
  j going out with friends

3 a We don't go to work on Saturdays.
  b We aren't policemen.
  c I don't have an expensive car.
  d We don't go to church on Sundays.
  e They don't like listening to music in the evenings.
  f You don't like playing tennis.

4 a I drink milk.
  b We are married.
  c You work on Mondays.
  d They have a new television.
  e We like swimming.
  f They like going out in the evenings.

5 a When do you like eating in restaurants?
  b When do you go to school/work?
  c When do you go swimming?
  d When do you go out with friends?
  e When do you have English lessons?

6 a in   b At   c on   d in   e to   f On
  g in   h On/to   i at   j in

8 (I'm from Ireland and) my husband, Pablo, is from Columbia. We
  live in a small house in Dublin. We have one son. I'm a doctor
  and Pablo is a Spanish teacher. We like cooking and dancing.

9 It's half past eight./It's quarter past two./It's quarter to twelve./It's
  twenty-five to one./It's five past twelve.

10

12 a We work on Saturdays.
  b We don't work on Sundays.
  c We don't like reading in the evenings.
  d We like listening to music.
  e We don't like playing tennis at weekends.
  f We like watching television.

UNIT 8

1 Journalist: He has a computer./He works at home.
  Footballer: He drives to work./He trains a lot./He plays matches.
  Taxi driver: He sometimes works at night./He drives a lot./He
    meets a lot of people.

2 a does   b Do   c do   d Does   e do
  f does   g Do   h Does

3 a cooks   b has   c drive   d do   e do
  f have   g like

4 a Yes, she does.   b No, he doesn't.
  c Yes, he does.   d No, she doesn't.
  e Yes, he does.   f No, she doesn't.
  g No, he doesn't.   h No, she doesn't.

5 a has   b likes   c likes   d eats   e likes

6 is/live/is/works/reads/writes/has/work/have/drive/
  walk/plays/go/go/cook

7 a doesn't   b do   c don't   d doesn't
  e does   f don't   g do   h does

8 When does Tracy get up? She gets up at quarter to eight.
  When does Lee go to work? He goes to work at quarter past seven.
  When does Tracy go to work? She goes to work at nine o'clock.
  When does Lee have lunch? He has lunch at half past twelve.
  When does Lee arrive home? He arrives home at twenty past four.
  When does Tracy arrive home? She arrives home at twenty-five to
    six.

9 b train   c bike   d car   e bus
  f motorbike   g plane

10 1 I'm sorry   2 Excuse me   3 Excuse me/I'm sorry

UNIT 9

1 b has breakfast   c leaves/twenty-five past eight
  d teaches   e has   f leaves/half past four   g arrives

2 a – 3, c – 1, d – 2, e – 4

Photocopiable © OXFORD UNIVERSITY PRESS

3
a   Who works on Saturdays? 2
b   What does Oliver do? 5
c   Why does he walk to work? 4
d   When does she leave home? 1

4
b   He lives in Glasgow.
c   He gets up at half past seven.
d   Because he likes talking to people.
e   At weekends he visits his mother.

5
a   doesn't have   b   doesn't start   c   doesn't have
d   doesn't visit   e   doesn't live

7
a   like   b   have   c   live   d   does
e   visit   f   get up   g   like

8
a   The train doesn't leave at quarter to one.
b   Raoul doesn't go to work by bike.
c   Ramiro and Raquel don't eat eggs for breakfast.
d   Lorena's sister isn't a travel agent.
e   Piet doesn't leave work at half past four.
f   Oliver and Neville don't like playing tennis.
g   This book isn't very interesting.
h   Lídia doesn't work in a bank.
i   We aren't policemen.
j   Erol isn't married.

9
a   Lolita likes working in a bank.
b   Manuel and Pilar go out at weekends.
c   They're from Britain.
d   Chris leaves work at six o'clock.
e   His name's Stefan.
f   Lourdes has a television.
g   The school's in the centre of the city.
h   Martin and Anne like their jobs.

10
b   at   c   at   d   for   e   on   f   on   g   at
h   to   for

11 Nice/you/How/bad/Goodbye/Have/nice/Same/ Thanks/on

12
b   go to bed   c   stop   d   old   e   father
f   leave   g   play   h   sister   i   early
j   expensive

14
```
W O R K S       S I X         W H Y
        T       T               H
    S E C O N D A R Y S C H O O L
    P       P       R
    E       I N T E R E S T I N G
E A R L Y               W
    K   E               E
        A               L
        V   E X P E N S I V E
        E               E
        U S U A L L Y
```

UNIT 10

1
B   dining room   C   kitchen   D   bedroom
E   bathroom   F   garden

2
2   sofa   3   armchair   4   table   5   chair
6   cooker   7   fridge   8   bed   9   picture
10 lamp   11 bath   12 toilet   13 cat
14 car   15 tree   16 bicycle

4
a   No, there isn't.   b   No, there aren't.
c   Yes, there is.   d   No, there aren't.
e   Yes, there is.   f   Yes, there are.

5
a   Is there a television in the living room? Yes, there is.
b   Are there any chairs in the kitchen? No, there aren't.
c   Are there any cats in the garden? Yes, there are.
d   Is there a television in the dining room? No, there isn't.
e   Are there any armchairs in the bedroom? No, there aren't.
f   Is there a table in the dining room? Yes, there is.

6 Is there a table in the garden? No, there isn't.
Is this your pencil? Yes, it is.
Is Corinne from Britain? No, she isn't.
Are there any flowers on the table? Yes, there are.
Are Kim and Frances married? Yes, they are.

7
2   red, orange, green   3   brown   4   white
5   blue   6   black   7   grey

8
b   Yes, it does.   c   They're blue.   d   Yes, there is.
e   They sit in the living room and watch television or listen to music.
f   No, it isn't.   g   They have lunch in the dining room.
h   Yes, there are.   i   Yes, they are.

10
b   at   c   in   d   on   e   from   f   for   g   at
h   by   i   in   j   in   k   on/in

11 First column: lovely, Tuesday, children
Second column: cassette, antique
Third column: secondary, interesting, secretary
Fourth column: assistant, banana
Fifth column: afternoon

13 Good afternoon./Afternoon./I'd like these envelopes, please./ That's 85p, please./Here you are . . . Thank you./ Thank you.

14 Could/have/please/That's/Here/Thank/Thanks

UNIT 11

1
a   It's £9.99.   b   They're £9.90 (for five).
c   It's £6.59.   d   They're £4.99 (for three).
e   It's £9.99.   f   It's £5.30.

2 two pounds ninety-nine – £2.99, five p – 5p, fifteen pounds fifty-five – £15.55, forty-three p – 43p, one pound sixty-eight – £1.68, sixty p – 60p, five pounds seventy-two – £5.72, three pounds eighty-one – £3.81, ninety-eight p – 98p, seventy-five p – 75p, seventeen p – 17p, fifty-eight p – 58p, ninety-nine pounds – £99, twenty-six pounds forty-seven – £26.47

3
a   three pounds thirty eight   b   one pound four
c   ten pounds   d   ninety-four p
e   eleven pounds ninety-eight   f   forty-nine p
g   ninety-one pounds twenty   h   two pounds fourteen
i   eighty-eight p   j   sixty-five pounds fifty

4 Can I have/Anything else?/Good afternoon./How much is/I'm sorry./No, thanks./Can I help you?/How much are/That's £15.20, please.

5 Yes, can I have a ham salad, please?/Certainly, here you are. Anything else?/Yes. An orange juice./That's £4.10./Here you are …. Thanks./Thanks.

6 b Here you are.
c Can I have a ham sandwich, please?
d Anything to drink?
e How much is that?

8 Possible answers
a I don't have a radio/cassette/video.
b she doesn't like watching television/going to restaurants.
c he doesn't like oranges/bananas.
d they don't like playing tennis/swimming.
e she doesn't have a cat.

9 Food and drink: chips, ham salad, orange juice, sandwich, tea
Colours: black, blue, green, red, white, yellow
Jobs: baker, dentist, journalist, nurse, secretary, shop assistant
Rooms: bathroom, bedroom, dining room, kitchen, living room
Places: bank, factory, hospital, post office, restaurant, travel agency

11 a ✗ b a c ✗ d the e a f a
g ✗ h the i ✗

UNIT 12

1 b July (7) c April (4) d December (12)
e October (10) f February (2) g September (9)
h June (6) i August (8) j March (3)
k November (11) l May (5)

2 b spring c winter d autumn

3 4 They usually stay in a small house or a flat by the sea, but sometimes they stay in a hotel.
5 Joshua goes swimming …
3 They usually have sandwiches for lunch …
2 In the afternoons they walk … in the park.
6 In the evenings they often go to the cinema …

4 b often c never d sometimes e usually

5 a Liz often goes out for dinner at weekends.
b Do you often go to the cinema?
c I sometimes go to France for two weeks in July.
d We never drive to work.
e Does she usually have lunch with you?
f Silvio usually goes dancing with Leontina on Saturdays.
g Does Henry learn English at weekends?
h Is it usually cold in November?

7 a do b do c does d does e do

8 a day b love c new d I e my
f dance g usually

9 a ✗ b ✗ c ✔ d ✗ e ✗ f ✔

11 a wet b cold c warm d hot

12 a wind b sun c snow d rain e fog

13 a December b red c reading
d very e Monday f notebook
g weekend h garden

14 Yes, can I change some traveller's cheques, please?/Yes, of course. How much do you want to change?/£80./Can I see your passport, please?…/Here you are./Thank you. Can you sign here, please? That's twenty, forty, sixty, eighty pounds./Thank you. Goodbye.

STOP AND CHECK 2

1 b She's a doctor. c They get up at seven o'clock.
d They visit their friends. e They go to the beach.
f Because it's very cold.

2 c Yes, there are. d Yes, usually.
e Yes, she does. f Yes, always.
g No, never. h Yes, they do.

3 to/How/not/at/has/on/Good/help/a/of/an/else/No/on/When/At

4 Months: February, October
Bank: money, traveller's cheque.
Seasons: winter, autumn, spring
Food & drink: coffee, salad, mineral water
Colours: blue, green, brown
Rooms: toilet, kitchen, living room
Furniture: armchair, sofa, table

Oxford University Press, Walton Street, Oxford OX2 6DP

Oxford New York
Athens Auckland Bangkok Bogota Bombay
Buenos Aires Calcutta Cape Town Dar es Salaam
Delhi Florence Hong Kong Istanbul Karachi
Kuala Lumpur Madras Madrid Melbourne
Mexico City Nairobi Paris Singapore
Taipei Tokyo Toronto

and associated companies in
Berlin Ibadan

OXFORD and OXFORD ENGLISH are trade marks of Oxford University Press

ISBN 0 19 435723 6

© Oxford University Press

First published 1995
Third impression 1996

Designed by Keith Shaw, Threefold Design, Oxford

Illustrations by:
Katherine Baxter
Valerie Falla

Printed in Malta by Interprint Ltd.